The Thrill
of the Hunt

The Thrill of the Hunt

Life Lessons from a Puppy

Rob Crawford

ISBN: 978-0-578-57816-3

Cover and author photos by Ryan Read.
Page design by Win-Win Words LLC

Printed in the United States of America

To the Maker,
And to the makers.

Contents

Acknowledgments

FIRST AND FOREMOST, I WANT TO PRAISE AND THANK MY MAKER, from whom all blessings flow, who forever invites me deeper into the mystery of His great love. This Life has been wilder than any I could have ever asked for, and I'm grateful for the grace and mercy that cover me when I ask for less and not more.

Next, I want to thank my parents for raising me up in the way I should go, so that when I am old, I will not depart from it.

I owe a lifelong debt of gratitude to the surgeons, nurses, paramedics, and physical therapists who nurtured me back to health, doing so with the utmost grace and tenderness. Their compassion is something that is never far from my mind.

I want to thank the friends and family who have walked with me along my journey. I'll never fully be able to say just how much you've meant to me, but this book is the first of many attempts to do so.

Finally, thank you to everyone who emotionally and financially contributed to this project. I've done my best to list their blessed names below, but you know who you are.

Charlie, Adams, TBA, Wes & Katie Crawford; Tim Crawford; Michele O'Connor; Hellen & Bob Baker; Charlie & Thelma Crawford; Bill & Chrissy Haslam; Lee & Malissa Scruggs; David & Martha Reynolds ; Herbert & Cary Slatery;

The Thrill of the Hunt

Greg and Jeannine Adams; Dave & Karen Baumgartner; Trey & Hailey Alley; Carter Miller; Rodney & Lynn Miller; Johan and Katie Larsen; Pamela Schoenewaldt; Pablo Giacopelli; Shannon Burke; Mike Towle; Hunter & Kristina Wright; Brad Burling; Priscilla Molina; Maddie Lane; Brian McNew; Greg Korlin; Michael & Lizzie Nelson; Chaz Ayton; Alix Freeman; Allen & Eric Doty; Alex & Jamie Oliver; Mitchell Tenpenny; Adam & Mari McCall; Jordan Howell; Daniel Walden; Derrick Furlow Jr.; Ryan & Kayla Read; Ryan & Laura Dailey; Barry & Debbie Faust; Drew & Haley Wall; Preston & Barbara Fields; Matthew Debardelaben; Carmen Depaoli; Makayla Waits; Kathleen & Clayton Stroop; Mr. & Mrs. Tommy Stroop; Jason Shoemacher; Nolan & Sara Gray; Rudy Uhde; Courtney Durbin; The Deiblers; Caroline Brannen; Tyler Stooksbury; Beau Patton; Carlos Lamkin; Cameron King; Brittney Harris; Rory McMillan; Greg Brown; Kaitlyn Rodabaugh; Malissa Cunningham; Sarah Hill; Juby Whitney Webb; Ryan & Maggie McMillan; Clint Smith; Tyler Grobowsky; Morgan & Courtney Hutcheson; John Keck; Joy Lauderdale; Laura Roberts; Mike Hallman; Courtney Daly; Uncle Bill & Aunt Lisa; Jay Crawford; Patrick and Olivia Flynn; David & Sandy Durbin; Nadim Jubran; Jonathan Kerr; Kaelea Wilson; Geysel Gomez; Alexandra Knight; Harrison Collins; Rick Vern; Spencer Waters; Madison Boyd; Louise Hebbeler, and Will Mabry.

Preface

"Perhaps time's definition of coal is the diamond."
— Kahlil Gibran

THE TRUTH IS—WE ARE UTTERLY HUMAN. If that doesn't sit well with you, I recommend that you find the nearest fire pit and ceremonially burn this book. For those of you reading this on a digital platform, I suggest simply deleting the file. We are human, which combines wretched brokenness with the most profound beauty in all of creation.

If you're reading this book, I'm going to assume you have a basic knowledge of (or at least an interest in) the scriptures many of us have grown up with. King David marvels at God's design of humanity by saying:

> I thank you, High God—you're breathtaking!
> Body and soul, I am marvelously made!
> I worship in adoration—what a creation!
> You know me inside and out, you know every
> bone in my body;
> You know exactly how I was made, bit by bit,
> how I was sculpted from *nothing into some-
> thing.*[Emphasis author]
> — *Psalms 139:14-16* (MSG)

King David also suffered from deep bouts of depression, cursing his existence and wondering where God was in the midst of his many battles. I wonder how a man of David's stature could, in one moment, praise God's immaculate design only to doubt his goodness in the next. Even more curiously, why would God claim David to be a man after His own heart, despite the fact that modern psychiatry would likely diagnose him as bipolar?

Many of us can relate to this double life. At times, we might feel like a mighty warrior for God's name. In others, we completely forget God's promises, leaving us weak, discouraged, and alone. Who is this God who toys with our emotions, and why would He do that to the children He claims to love?

Perhaps more urgently, you might be wondering why you picked up a book about dogs and are now reading about King David's mental instability. Well, I believe we have much to learn from our relationship with these four-legged, non-speaking companions we hold in such high regard. After all, the domesticated dog is only a slight genetic deviation from its cousin, the ravaging wolf. Yet we claim that a dog is man's best friend, often treating them as members of our family.

For a creature that sheds, barks, whines, soils the carpet, chews holes in the drywall, requires daily food and water (on top of costly vet bills after they actually swallow the drywall), that's quite a leap up the totem pole if you ask me. I'm speaking, of course, for those of us who invite our dogs into our home rather than leave them chained to the tree outside.

As I consider my own messy life, how it's riddled with sin and addiction, how I plead for guidance only to defiantly ignore it a moment later, I wonder how God feels about my wretched humanity. Does He grow weary of my requests and complaints? Perhaps it would be better to chain me to the tree outside His home, but what kind of life would that be?

As we examine our place before the Creator of the universe, let's keep in mind that we are cursed to toil the earth to which we have been sent, yet at the same time we're invited into God's masterful plan to save all mankind from our own wickedness. What did we do to deserve such great love as to be invited into our Master's home, even to dine with him *at* His dinner table?

Before we go any further, let me be clear about one fundamental (yet easily forgotten) thing that will continue to surface throughout our time together—God does not love us for *anything* we've done or could ever hope to do. God loves us because of who *He* is. He loves us because of *His* nature, and it is the same unconditional, loving nature of a dog that has inspired me to write this book. So here we find ourselves, amidst these two unconditionally loving beings, and I implore you to examine this peculiar dynamic in a playful manner.

Honest, relentless self-examination is painful only if we forget the aforementioned nature of God's love. Therefore, let's also remember that God already knows everything we've done and will do, as well as the motives behind them—motives that are often shameful and repulsive. This is the story of my coming to terms with this beautiful reality of God's infinitely free love and how I could not escape it. I share these insights in hope they might encourage you to see yourself in the same light God sees you, adores you, and yearns to be in relationship with you.

MOST OF US DON'T LIKE being bound to our humanity. Sound familiar? It should. Adam and Eve weren't married to the idea, either. While it was impossible for them to know what would befall creation if they ignored this reality, they chose to be their own masters, altering the course of mankind forever.

The Thrill of the Hunt

In the blink of an eye, Adam and Eve digressed from eternal to mortal beings; they had to leave the garden that was made for their enjoyment. Ever since that day, we've been searching for the entrance back into that paradise—back to the life in which we didn't have to work in order to fill our bellies. In that place, we could but lift a hand to pluck an almost infinite variety of fruits (all but one, of course). But we had to taste that one forbidden fruit, and ever since then we've been scratching behind our ears, wondering why all the fruit in the wilderness has a hint of bitterness to it. But God promises to lead us, through proper training, out of our childish defiance and into maturity, where we learn a beautiful paradox.

MY FAMILY GREW UP WITH a German shorthaired pointer (GSP). We called him Chip because of his brown ticking

Me as a boy with our dog Chip, named after Atlanta Braves star Chipper Jones.

That's me in front with the baseball cap, with my brothers Wes (left) and Tim (top right), along with our dog Chip.

that, to any six-year-old, resembled chocolate chips. We also got him in '95, the same year that baseball superstar Chipper Jones led the Atlanta Braves to their only World Series championship in the last sixty years. RIP Braves. I didn't realize how influential my relationship with Chip was to my boyhood until many years later. Needless to say, we had quite a bond, and while he did not lead the Braves to another championship, he did lead a full and fulfilling life.

I got my second GSP puppy in 2012, when I was a twenty-four-year-old hippie wannabe with little to no reason to be raising a dog. I named him Chipper, probably after some subconscious desire to recreate my childhood bond. Chipper's appearance was practically identical to Chip Sr. Sadly, my emotional state was practically identical to that of my six-year-old self. Although Chipper and I had plenty of great moments and insights together over the next year, our

Me later in my hippie-hair years, with my second dog, Chipper (or Chip Jr.).

time together would come to an abrupt end.

You might not be familiar with the GSP breed, but they are a force to be reckoned with. They were bred for bird hunting, and their high energy level enables them to comb a quail field for ten nonstop hours a day. Their puppyhood energy levels astonishingly are sustained well into their sixth year, when they finally begin to relax a bit and let the younger pups do the grunt work.

I don't tell you this to deter you from the breed. They are brilliant dogs, gentle as all get out; perhaps my favorite feature—they are practically speechless. The only time they break their stoic silence is during playtime with other dogs, when they utilize their extensive vocabulary, consisting largely of dramatically drawn-out vowels.

In May 2016, after a tumultuous couple of years, I got Yonah, my third GSP. I know, why not punctuate emotional catastrophe with arguably the most hyper breed on the planet? Brilliant! Believe it or not, I'd grown significantly since my last pup four years prior, and something clicked with this one.

Most of the insights we'll explore here come from my time with Yonah. But, interestingly enough, I first had the idea to write this book with Chipper. That's when I began to realize how profoundly I'd been influenced by Chip Sr. I attribute much of my personality to the boyhood days of squirrel hunting in the backwoods with Chip Sr., where the groundwork for manhood was laid out before me, far unbeknownst to me . . . or Chip Sr. RIP.

I'm thirty years old as I write this and have barely scratched the surface of whom God has made me to be. But of all the things I've learned in my adult life, the most important insight by far has been God's insistence on my remaining a child. Not a whiny, snotty, diaper-spoiling child of mind, but a beautiful, trusting, adoring child at heart.

So . . . if you're willing to entertain this curious notion, let's take a walk. The trail ahead is overgrown, and we might very well lose our bearings. But so what? What's a good adventure if you don't get lost once or twice along the way?

The Thrill
of the Hunt

1

Puppyhood

"The older dog don't ginerally raise no ruction, hit's the younger one that's ill."

— Horace Kephart, *Our Southern Highlanders* [1]

OH, THE JOYS OF PUPPYHOOD. I don't think I've ever experienced such a sweet season of life peppered with the most perplexing reminders that I have no control over this wild animal.

If you have a rescued dog or are thinking about rescuing a dog, good on you. In my experience, that decision reflects the condition of the rescuer more than it does their compassion toward the rescued.

I've heard it said that there is no such thing as a bad dog, only a bad dog owner. And one of the many reasons we have so many bad dog owners is that an owner neglects his or her due diligence in finding a breed to match his or her lifestyle. There's nothing inherently wrong with coming home from work and watching Netflix all afternoon, but it's probably not wise for you to have a Boxer that requires hours of daily exercise. If you enjoy peace and quiet in your home, I recommend staying away from shepherding, as they tend to, ya know, guard your home and alert you of any and all potential dangers.

If you take the route of finding your pup through a breeder, you'll likely spend months searching for the right fit. With certain breeds in high demand, it's quite common to be put on a waiting list. After you match with the right breeder, you immediately go to the nearest pet store and drop a couple hundred bucks on what you believe will suffice through the stages of puppyhood. Perhaps you have to wait for the puppy to come of age, usually seven to ten weeks before they are ready to part from their mother. In Yonah's case, I found him through the breeder's website but was unable to make the ten-hour drive for another month and a half.

The breeder generously sent me videos during my waiting period, and I watched his litter of six gradually reduce in number. When the weekend finally came for me to make the drive, I arrived at the breeder's farm to find Yonah alone in a little playpen. I wondered if he had any idea that he was the first to be chosen and the last to be picked up. But there he was, twelve weeks old, and more than ready for his world to expand outside the waist-high playpen.

I chatted with the breeder for half an hour, then Yonah and I jumped into the car and began the long trek to our new life together. Two miles down the road, I looked in the rear view of my station wagon to find a fresh pile of undigested dog food which was, quite literally, half the size of his body mass. It was then I realized he'd never been in a car before. Just like me, he suffered from car sickness. We stopped at the next gas station and I did my best to clean the mess with the paper towels offered at the gas pump. Don't worry; I did *not* recycle the undigested dog food, but I thought about it.

We got back on the road and, for the next several hours, he patiently looked out the back window at the vast new world into which he was entering. I smiled, knowing both of our lives had just taken a significant turn.

Four photos from my first day with Yonah. Top left, in his playpen as I get ready to pick him up. Top right, looking out the back window on his trip to his new home. Bottom left, resting on a towel on the floor of my car. Bottom right, now in his new home, in my cabin.

The Thrill of the Hunt

LIFE IS JUST BETTER WITH a puppy. Sure, it comes with its share of newfound responsibilities such as cleaning pee off the rug, removing dangerous objects out of his mouth, trying not to crush him beneath every step, and many other measures to keep that puppy breath flowing in and out of his lungs. OK, life with a puppy is exhausting, but c'mon! It's basically endless hours of entertainment broken up only by sweet puppy naps in my lap. For the first twelve weeks of Yonah's life, his world had been confined to a playpen the size of a bathtub. Needless to say, watching him explore his brave new world was riveting.

His nose was coming alive, and he followed it everywhere. He was a puppy through and through; more so, he was *my* puppy. We went everywhere together—sauntering through the woods, driving through the countryside (much to his dismay), and kayaking the French Broad River.

The cabin I had recently moved into was a paradise for us both. It was, coincidentally, situated less than a mile from Seven Islands Bird Sanctuary. I didn't plan it this way, but my goodness, did Yonah hit the jackpot! A bird dog in a bird sanctuary is a sight to behold.

Our first weekend together, I decided it was time for his first swim lesson. My previous two GSPs had been great swimmers, though neither was particularly motivated to jump into the river. Yonah was no different. I waded into the shallow water and beckoned him to follow, but he sat there whimpering on the shoreline. He wanted to be close to me, but he was terrified of the murky river water.

IT HAD BEEN AN EMOTIONALLY exhausting few years leading up to my decision to get Yonah. I'll talk in more depth about those events in later chapters; for now, suffice it to say that I'd recently been engaged to be married (twice, in fact, to the

More photos of Yonah and me, in our first few weeks together. Pretty much everywhere I went, he went . . . and vice versa.

same girl). That relationship ended catastrophically within months of my parents' finalizing their divorce after a presumably spotless thirty-seven years together.

Needless to say, I was exhausted. Everything that I thought I knew about life, love, and relationships had just been turned on its head, and I was left deeply wounded and confused.

A buddy of mine had a cabin outside of town. When I was still engaged, he had offered to turn his basement into an apartment for me and my soon-to-be-bride. I called him a couple weeks after everything went down and explained she was out of the picture, but that I could really use some country living in my life.

"Just one thing, though. How do you feel about a puppy?"

"C'mon," he said.

Yonah and I moved in about a month later and we were in paradise. The cabin sits on eight acres of farmland, but it's surrounded by hundreds more. It's mostly wooded, but there's also plenty of pasture to roam. During the weekdays, I would start and end every day in complete bliss watching Yonah learn to use his nose. On the weekends, we would paddle out to the bird sanctuary and let him roam to his heart's content.

On this island paradise in the foothills of Appalachia, Yonah would disappear for hours on end. As he was not yet keen on swimming, I had no reason to worry about him running off, which allowed me to just sit . . . and be. Lying in the gentle rapids of the cool mountain waters, I let the sun warm my flesh and soul.

On one occasion, I remember thinking, *I forgot how pleasant this is; how perfect!* Having lived and worked on the same city block for the previous three years, I had gotten in the habit of neglecting short day trips like this, usually in favor of something more convenient (such as a beer garden).

As it often does, my mind began to sabotage itself and wreck the stillness around me. My train of thought followed a familiar pattern, sounding something like:

If I'd remembered to cherish moments like this, maybe I'd still be engaged. We might even be married by now.

If my marriage ends up like my parents', do I even want to be married?

If I could just be better, maybe she'd take me back.

Why am I such an idiot?

How could I have been so selfish?

How can she be so selfish?

My mind quickly descended into a tumultuous series of "what ifs" and "whys," and my heart found its paradise replaced with an all-too-familiar prison cell.

All of a sudden, my thoughts were shattered by a noise. I turned to find a doe splashing through the water heading straight toward me. Finding me in her path (and looking every bit as surprised as I must have looked), she changed course and darted back into the woods. I looked back to find Yonah barreling through the brush in hot pursuit. His awkward puppy legs got crossed up and he tumbled down the bank into the stream. Without skipping a beat, he picked up the chase and was just about to disappear into the brush when I called his name. He came over and laid down in the water beside me, out of breath and happy as I'd ever seen him.

An overwhelming sense of peace rose up from my heart and my exhausted mind found rest. *"Child, just be here with me in this moment,"* God whispered. *"If you spend the rest of your life trying to answer these questions, you'll miss what I have for you here and now."*

"You're right," I whispered back. *"Thank you."*
Time for another swim lesson.

IT WAS TURNING OUT TO be the best summer I'd had in years. Every week was filled with new adventures. Because of all the inspiration that naturally comes with adventure, my professional life as a writer was bursting at the seams with creativity. *Finally,* I thought, *life is looking up.*

In the middle of that August, I got an invite up to my buddy's lake house on a mystical lake in the mountains of North Carolina. The geography up there is breathtaking. Nearly two hundred quaint cabins and vacation homes are nestled into its northern bank. The south shore is preserved as a state park and is just as pristine and primitive as it's been for decades since the dam was built in 1928.

Because of the steep banks, the lakefront homes are practically hanging over the waterline (at least their patio decks are). Ever since I was about thirteen, I have identified myself as a thrill seeker. As a result, I have developed a terrible habit of cliff jumping. If there's a cliff to jump off, I'm going to jump off it. Always have and in a certain sense, I always will. In this case, the cliff was a wooden patio that sits some fifty feet above the water.

My buddy, who's also a thrill seeker, had owned the house for nearly two years. Every weekend we'd been up there together, we would notice each other silently entertaining the possibility of making the jump. Prior contemplations had been abandoned due to a tree limb situated smack dab in the middle of the most feasible launch zone. We'd shake our head and let go of the thought until next time. But when I came for that particular visit, I was happy to find the tree limb had been clipped to present a better view of the sunrise along the southeast shore.

As was customary, we found ourselves out on his deck, drooling over the possibility. I looked over, wondering if he was thinking what I was thinking. He was not.

"Not this weekend," he said sternly.

There was a group of twelve or so on their way up to enjoy the weekend, and he didn't want to turn this into a stunt. That was perfectly understandable. I said I wouldn't, and that was that. Our friends soon arrived and the weekend festivities began.

The next afternoon I found myself on the patio playing guitar with another friend. The rest of the group were either out on the boat or napping in the various rooms of the lake house. My friend and I had spent half an hour or so figuring out how to play Leon Bridges's "River." It's a beautiful song of prayer that he and I had grown fond of singing together. The chorus is a simple plea to God:

"Take me to your river.

"I want to go.

"Take me to your river;

"I want to know."

All of a sudden, I realized my opportunity. The jump had been staring a hole through my pride for two years now. With no one around to watch, it was the perfect time to get it out of my system and be done with it.

Without hesitation, I stood up and handed my buddy the guitar. He assumed I was going inside and picked up playing the song where I'd left off. But instead of going inside, I did a Tennessee two-step over to the railing, hoisted myself up, and spread my wings . . . only to find that my wings weren't wings. They were arms, and the railing was, in fact, *not* a secure launch ramp.

My legs pushed with such force that the railing gave way and I plummeted to the waterline below, quickly discovering that this particular waterline felt eerily similar to a bed of rocks.

And there I was, gasping for breath on the rocks along the shoreline. Just like that, everything had changed. I was a mutinous pirate who had just walked the plank. Now I floated in the open seas, watching the ship of my old life sailing on without me. I remember being fascinated, or perhaps 'bewildered' is a better word, with the realization: *Oh, so this is what it takes.*

You see, for years leading up to this moment, I was keenly aware that my life was *not* what I thought it should be or what God wanted it to be. I'd tried every way I knew to be different, but to no avail. I'd begun to hate myself deeply, and in the dead of many nights, I often cried out to God to do 'whatever it takes' to get my attention. *You'd better show yourself, God, 'cuz I'm looking, and I'm listening! But I'm not seeing, and I'm not hearing!*

There I was. I couldn't move my legs, and my whole lower body was tingling the way it feels when your hand falls asleep. *So, this is what it takes. OK, you have my attention*, I thought as I lowered myself down into the water and floated weightlessly as unwitting boaters cruised by. I lay there and looked back up at the railing from which I had just stepped off.

My buddy Jordan (whose name is all too perfect for the song I was just singing and the river I'd just been baptized in) rushed to my side and did his best to stabilize my back as the waves of boating passersby crashed along the shoreline. All I wanted was to curl up in a ball and go to sleep, which is precisely the thing you should not do when your nervous system is going into shock. I kept closing my eyes, and Jordan continued to force them back open. He threatened to kiss me if I closed my eyes one more time. I often wonder what would have happened if I drifted into unconsciousness at that moment. I imagine I could have died or possibly slipped into a coma. It might have been one of those stories you hear about people dying and going to heaven, only to come back to life some indefinite amount of time later.

Regardless, Jordan's threat to kiss me apparently did the trick because he kept me awake for the half hour it took for the paramedics to arrive on the scene. They determined that the incline of the shoreline was far too steep to carry me up in a position that wouldn't cause more damage to my spine. That's when they loaded me onto a pontoon boat and took me to the marina, where I was quickly transported by ambulance to the nearby helicopter pad.

As we waited for the airlift, I begged them not to load me onto the helicopter. The paramedic insisted it would be impossible to safely transport me in an ambulance. The nearest hospital was two hours away, and the road to it is notoriously known as "the Tail of the Dragon" and boasts 318 hairpin turns in a span of eleven miles. Motorcyclists travel from every corner of the world to ride this stretch of highway; unfortunately, dozens of cyclists each year are involved in accidents, which also explains why there is a helicopter pad in the area.

When the paramedics asked why I was so reluctant to ride the helicopter, I told them that the airlift would inevitably take me to the University of Tennessee Medical Center, where my ex-fiancée was employed as a nurse on the trauma floor. She would inevitably be there working on the trauma unit that would receive me. If that doesn't blow your mind, what if I told you that a year prior, the moment she and I found out she was going to be a trauma nurse, I knew I would one day end up on her floor?

Well, fate had its way. I pleaded with them not to bring

my prophecy to fruition, but there was no point. What was I going to do, get up and run away?

MY ACCIDENT RANG ACROSS MY life like a bell in a town square. Actually, it was more like a *Tom & Jerry* cartoon in which Jerry would hold a metal bowl over Tom's head and smack it with a wooden spoon, sending Tom into a seizure.

After being airlifted to UT Medical Center, I was surprised to find a group of friends and family already waiting for me. My ex-fiancée was, of course, there to greet me as well, smiling brightly as always. We all shared a few laughs and a few cries, but there was a single question that lingered in the room undeniably—"Can he still walk?" All we knew up to that point was that I was in "stable condition," which apparently meant something else to the doctors and nurses.

Of course, I'm stable, I thought, *I can't move my legs so I'm clearly not going anywhere.*

You'll have to forgive my making light of the incident. I'm not sure if it was shock, a defense mechanism, or just plain perplexity, but I remember being in good spirits the entire time. It wasn't that I didn't care if I would be able to walk again; I simply had a peace about the situation that's difficult to describe. If the first thought after my crash landing was one of enlightenment, I distinctly remember the second thought being one of resolve. I had desired *lasting* change for nearly a decade and every attempt faded into the past with the rest of them. But this . . . this was different, and I knew it. Whether I would walk out of the hospital or never take another step, I knew that life had dramatically changed.

The initial rounds of scans and MRIs determined that I had suffered a burst fracture in my L1 and L2 vertebrae, along with a fractured pelvis and several ribs. The medical staff scheduled my surgery for two days later, though I was in and out of consciousness for the next several days.

I do recall the most bone-chilling degree of pain, despite the morphine coursing through my veins, along with the deepest level of thirst I ever hope to experience. Right before I went under for surgery, I remember begging for a drink of water. For medical purposes, they weren't able to oblige, but they sought to comfort me with a damp sponge.

"I thirst! I thirst!" I cried out choking back tears. I had a hard time not thinking of another guy I know who cried out from thirst and was given vinegar from a cloth. My thirst felt petty in comparison. But that's all I could muster up in my delirium.

"I thirst. I thirst." Maybe that was the morphine talking. Then again, maybe it was something more.

DURING THE SURGERY, MY NEUROSURGEON (God bless him) had to remove bone shrapnel from the vertebrae that had shattered and splintered up and down my spinal cord. He then restructured my spine with a series of rods that would fuse with my vertebrae, and bam! Good as new, or was it *Good as it's gonna be?* I forget. Either way, the good news was that I had an incomplete spinal cord injury (it was not completely severed), meaning it was possible I could learn to walk again.

A few days later, the physical therapists brought a walker into my room. It might as well have been a bobsled.

"What the hell do you expect me to do with that?" I exclaimed.

"Well, it *is* a walker, so . . . we want you to try and walk," replied one of the physical-therapy students employed by the university hospital.

"Y'all *do* realize I broke my back three days ago, right?"

"We just want you to try."

With the *Chariots of Fire* theme song in my head, I gripped the walker and agonizingly stood to my feet. This was the first step into my new life.

A few days later I was transferred off the trauma floor and out of the hospital where a medical team had masterfully performed my surgery. My neurosurgeon came to say good-bye shortly before I was to be transferred to the rehabilitation center at another hospital.

I was surprised to hear I was one of his last cases at that hospital. He himself was transferring to a new hospital in another state. In that moment, I knew his hands and expert-ise were of divine providence that I will not soon forget. He wished me luck in my recovery, and I thanked him earnestly.

RELEARNING HOW TO WALK WAS a strange feeling, to say the least. My legs knew what they were supposed to do. One foot in front of the other, right? Easier said than done. As I began physical therapy, I remember being midstep and looking at a particular spot on the floor, saying, "OK, my foot is going to land right there." And by the time my foot touched the ground, it had landed some ten inches from where I intended.

I can't even take a proper step, I thought. *This is ridiculous!*

But it wasn't. My legs were so weak due to the nerve damage of my impact and the four weeks of lying in a hos-pital bed. My muscles had atrophied, making my sense of balance laughable.

After the frustrating therapy session, I retired to my hospital room and sat up in my bed. I couldn't stop staring at my swollen, immobile feet. I realized that, before my mishap, I had never so much as given a second thought to my mobility or my legs for that matter. I had no reason to; my legs had always been there, moving when I wanted them to and taking me where I thought I needed to go.

Now, I could barely wiggle my big toes. And even though I couldn't feel them, I appreciated them for the first time in my life.

My God, what else have I taken for granted?

Up until that point, there was very little that I hadn't taken for granted. I'm not talking about the various blessings we all take for granted in western society—religious freedom, education, a car that lets us drive to work every day, jobs that allow us to buy food. I'm talking about the universal blessings we take for granted every second of our lives: our eyes, our ears, our brain's ability to discern, lungs filling with air and hearts pumping the blood that carries oxygen to our organs.

How could I ever take these gifts for granted? But at the same time, how could I not? I'd never been without them, so why would I recognize, much less appreciate, them? For most of us, these senses and normal functions of the body are just a part of life. And if we're alive, surely, we're entitled to them, right?

Apparently not, because as my time at the rehab center progressed, I realized I was the only person on my floor who had even the possibility of learning how to walk again. The other twenty or so patients whom I interacted with had all suffered a complete spinal cord injury. Barring an absolute miracle, they were confined to a wheelchair for their future mobility.

It took my parents' divorce, my failed engagement, and, finally, my broken back to see how horrifyingly petty my sense of entitlement had become. In a moment of clarity, I realized that as a broken sinner, in truth, the only thing I'm actually entitled to is death—eternal separation from God. If that's all I'm entitled to, that means everything else is a gift— a beautiful, undeserved gift that God pours into every area of my life. The problem is, I'd been believing a lie that the world had told me from birth—that I need something outside of myself to be fulfilled, like a wife, a new job, or even something as unattainable as self-righteousness through behavior modification. I spent every moment of every day searching for it, and the craziest part is that as often as I found it, it had never fulfilled me, and I *still* kept searching. It's like I couldn't hear God's voice over the chatter of my mind telling me what I needed externally to feel whole on the inside.

I'VE SINCE MOVED FROM THAT enchanted cabin just outside of town, but I used to take Yonah directly across the street to our neighbors' pasture. It was significantly larger than the one on our property, and I could still keep an eye on him as he explored several hundred yards away. The pasture was divided by a row of pine trees, and I typically stood against the tree line and watched him comb the field.

My heart was filled with joy as I watched him dart back and forth in full gallop from one end of the field to the other. If his big ears weren't so floppy, I swear he'd have taken flight. I wondered what he was thinking . . . probably nothing. He's probably just happy to be out in the field with his dad close by. *I wish I could be that happy,* I often found myself thinking. More than anything, I was just excited for him to wear himself out so he'd sleep through the night.

One time, he was starting to explore a little too far away for my comfort, so I whistled for him and he came running back happily. But he suddenly stopped about forty yards off and looked around. I wondered what he was doing. I whistled softly, and his head whipped around looking for me before spontaneously taking off in the wrong direction. I whistled again, but he couldn't hear me over the jingling bells around his neck. Since I was standing motionless against the tree line, I realized he couldn't see me, and even though he wanted to find me, he wasn't willing to stop and really listen to where the sound was coming from.

In a moment, it all made so much sense. I hadn't been able to hear God's voice because I wasn't listening for it. I expected Him to be somewhere different or to show up in a more obvious way, when in fact, he was closer than I ever could have imagined. Furthermore, I was more concerned with what I needed than what was being said. For far too long and far too often, I had only been listening to the world around me, seeking its validation and affirmation and hoping to hear it declare I was lovable. I won't speak for you, but I live in a very conditional world, where I have to earn someone's love and respect. The problem is—when is it enough? When am I finally and irrevocably content with who the world says I am?

Like a held child who wants to be placed down so he can go play with his favorite toy, I would run off and be entertained for a short time, only to soon find out that there was no life in *that* toy. So, I'd set it down and go in search of the next thing, hoping it might have the life I was seeking. Out of His love for me, and with great patience, God let me go to those places of emptiness, knowing that one day I would realize there's no life there, or anywhere for that matter, apart from Him. But no matter where I run or how long I'm gone, He's right there with me, every step I take.

When I recall the eternal moments between stepping off the railing and falling to the rocks below, I felt God's firm grip around the scruff of my neck. Not that He compelled me to jump off the balcony, but that He was fully in control of my fall. And while I suffered a devastating blow, I was certain of His embrace. Finally, I knew. On my way to the inevitable rocks below, it's as if I could hear Him say, *"This is going to hurt. But trust me, it's for your good. I have some things I want to show you about your heart. Now sit back and try to relax. I got you, homie."*

In the neighbor's field that day, Yonah was eager to find me, but he wouldn't stop long enough to actually listen to my call. He just kept running from one side of the field to the other, figuring I would eventually appear. And just like Yonah's bells jingling around his neck, the empty promises of the world blocked my ability to hear God's voice in my life. Still, I kept running from one thing to the next, even running to seemingly good things such as Bible studies, Christian books, or small groups. Whatever it was, it can all be summed up as a restless squirming. In my efforts to grasp for things I thought I needed, I neglected everything that I already had.

Within the span of a year, my identity, my pride, and even my health had all been shattered. And now that I was practically immobile for twenty-three hours a day, I had nowhere to run. I was in diapers and relearning how to walk. My heart and body ached, and my mind fluttered with questions. The good thing about questions is that they warrant answers. And God has no shortage of answers if we are willing to learn to listen.

Now that my eyes had been opened (perhaps for the first time ever), I began to see life in an incredibly new and revolutionary way—one step at a time. Every step was a challenge, and every step was a victory. My heart was open to any and all opportunities to make progress in my recovery; believe me, there were plenty. My weak and broken body was no longer able to squirm, and my humiliation birthed humility. I was like a child in more ways than one, and that gift of the Spirit was sufficient unto the day.

Yonah was so excited to run through the open field that he had no idea he had just jumped over a fawn. (Look very closely, to the right side of the photo, about even with Yonah's ears.)

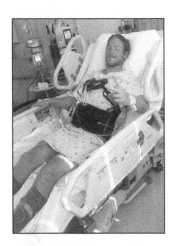 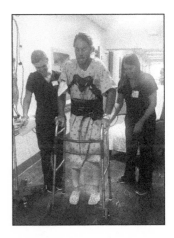

Left: My first time wearing green socks, although you can't tell it from the black and white format. Right: My first steps after the accident.

2

Discipline as Love

"Truly, that man is happy who has training from the hand of God: so do not let your heart be shut to the teaching of the Ruler of all. For He wounds, but He also binds up, He injures but He also heals."

— Job 5:17

H EALING IS A FASCINATING CONCEPT. It's a lot like watching paint dry, only the paint is battery acid and it's burning under your skin. Your body is painfully aware of the fact that something isn't right, but it's not like you can eat an extra bowl of Wheaties in the morning and suddenly you're a champion again (although Kellogg's marketing department might disagree).

After an adverse incident, it's quite natural for your mind to plot out a course of action to most efficiently return the body to its normal state of comfort. But in dealing with trauma, your world is turned upside down, and nothing looks the same. The body's routes of communication are in overdrive as the mind attempts to address the issue and shut off the alarm system. All this, of course, is taking place deep in the subconscious.

On the surface level, I was just wondering, *What the hell am I supposed to do now?* As I began the process of retraining my legs how to walk, I was eager to learn why God had chosen to spare them in the first place. All things considered,

I was lucky to be alive, even more so that I didn't end up in a wheelchair.

Even though using my legs was roughly the equivalent of trying to walk on a pair of carrots, I made up my mind to charge full steam ahead at my new life.

A nurse told me once about healing, "There's not much you can do to speed up the healing process, but the possibilities of prolonging it are innumerable."

"OK, so what are some of the things I shouldn't do?"

"Well, the most important thing is to not fall."

"Did that one already; won't do it again. Got it, what's next?"

"And definitely no sudden movements."

"I'm walking on carrots here; that shouldn't be a problem."

"OK, never heard that one before. Look, just do everything your therapist tells you to do and try not to overdo it. Your body naturally wants to heal. You just have to give it time. Trust the process."

Now, trusting the process . . . well, *that* is easier said than done.

FOR OUR FIRST FEW MONTHS together, I practically had to drag Yonah into the car. He viewed it with the same dreadful disdain set aside for monstrosities such as the vacuum cleaner and bath time. During the car rides, in fact, he drooled so excessively that I had to put him in the crate just to contain the havoc to one cubic yard. But month after month, he began to see that, while the car ride itself was nauseating, he grew less wary of the car and came to understand that the car meant adventure. He began to trust.

His fear of the water also began to gradually subside. We spent most of our free time on the river, and, barring any recent rain, the water between the islands stays pretty shallow. Often, his curiosity outgrew his fear. As long as he could feel the bottom of the river, he was happy to splash around the islands.

I couldn't help but wonder what he was so afraid of; the water is as clear as day, and, as far as I can tell, the most frightening thing you can see in the water is your own reflection. Then it hit me.

I heard God whisper, *"Rob, what is it about yourself that you continue to fear so much? Don't you know I love you?"*

"Of course, God. I know you've saved me. I know you love me," I whimpered back.

Another whisper—*"Do you?"*

I shrugged it off. You see, for years I'd felt a beckoning to step into the waters of life. It was faint, yet undeniable. I knew I was being called; we're all 'called' to do something with our lives, right? I just didn't know how to follow. Something was blocking me, and, try as I might, I simply could not pinpoint it.

I was stuck, paralyzed on the shore as my Master called me in. I sat there, whimpering prayers and begging to be swept away.

"Don't you want to swim?" God says.

"More than anything."

"Then c'mon, the water feels great. You'll love it."

"But I don't know how to swim," I reply.

"Doesn't matter; I'll teach you."

"But I can't see the bottom."

"Doesn't matter; I'll hold you."

"God, I'm scared."

"I know, but I'm with you. If you want to swim, you have to trust me."

"I can't." And every time I had ever been invited to swim

in the waters of life, I was left toeing the water out of fear. I tried to wrap my head around swimming and lived from my mind instead of living from my heart. Of course, I didn't know any of this at the time. That insight came from a whole other series of miracles.

THE FIRST SUNDAY AFTER BEING released from the hospital, I did as any good, pharisaic Christian would do and went back to church. I can just hear all the Southern Baptists out there, *"See, the Good Lord broke his back so he'd have to sit his butt in a church pew."*

In all sincerity, I had a rough road to recovery ahead, and I knew well enough to know I'd be needing a community for support. This one was going to be too big to take on alone.

That's when God led me to Ignition Church in downtown Knoxville (which has since changed its name to Maker City Church). I had actually been there before nearly four years earlier, and I found it to be showy and uncomfortable. But this time, something had changed. Maybe my heart was in a different spot; maybe the church had evolved. Whatever it was, I walked through the door and ran head on into a wall of love. 'Wall' is maybe not the best term because it implies a possibility of inclusion and exclusion. I only refer to it as a wall because its presence was abruptly perceivable and physically palpable.

The people at this church were beyond welcoming. I'm the sort of guy who likes to sneak in and observe a new space from a distance, but I soon found out this was not going to be possible. These people were so caring, so genuinely interested in hearing how I'd come through their door that morning, and their excitement was contagious.

Week after week, I timidly came back for more, and I was greeted with the same vigor. It's always awkward talking to strangers, especially at church where it's already awkward enough, and I'm not going to say these conversations were any less awkward. I was just amazed that no one seemed to care about the awkwardness. It was just sort of there, just like each one of us, and that was enough.

I had to know more about this comfort with the awkwardness, and it was through this amazing group of people that I began to observe the difference between following God with my mind and following God with my heart.

A MONTH OR SO LATER, I was sitting in the pasture letting Yonah get some exercise. It was a beautiful fall day and I had plenty to be grateful for, namely that I could walk down to the pasture in the first place. But something weighed heavily on my mind. Understandably, my accident had stirred up a whole mix of emotions, especially after seeing my ex-fiancée

Yonah and me in a pasture, next to a fire pit.

several times during my stay in the hospital. The sting of embarrassment and rejection was still fresh in my mind, and I began to resent myself for allowing such remorseful thoughts to cloud a beautiful autumn day.

"You know that I love you, right, Rob?"

Damn it, not this again. *"Yes, God, I know you love me."*

"Do you?"

"Yes!" I lashed back, *"I know that you love me. I know that you died for me. But I'm still sad because she . . . she doesn't . . . she doesn't love me . . . "*

I remember my thoughts stopping dead in the water. I was sitting there comparing the infinite love of the all-creating Father to the very finite love of His wounded and broken daughter—my ex-fiancée. Her rejection burned like hell. His free gift of acceptance . . . I had been rejecting. I was horrified.

"See, Rob, the reason you hurt so badly is because you allowed her love to enter your heart, while my love for you has always just remained in your mind like a fruit hanging from a tree, ready for you to pick at will. But my love doesn't work that way; it's meant to be consumed at a heart level and infiltrate every cell of your being."

I began to weep. It was all too true. Since childhood, my heart had been blown about by the winds of human acceptance, winds which are governed by the mind and its ability to perceive the safety therein. And here I was, blowing off the love of the Holy Spirit as it swirled all around me from the beginning of time.

This was the breakthrough I'd been begging for my entire life. This was the gift that I'd been too preoccupied to actually receive because of behavior modification. It's like I was too busy making my own birthday cake to attend the party my friend was throwing to celebrate me. It didn't come from the broken engagement, nor my parents' divorce, not even from my near-death experience. The breakthrough came from a gentle whisper from the Spirit, a persistent whisper that fluttered whenever I was quiet enough to actually hear it.

When I think about this moment, I always remember that scene from *Good Will Hunting,* where Robin Williams's character, Sean, compassionately confronts a wounded Matt Damon, Will. Standing across the office from one another, Sean repeatedly attempts to comfort his student because of the way his life has gone.

"It's not your fault," Sean says.

Will repeatedly brushes it off with a nod, *"I know."* To a less-caring therapist, Will's response would have been believable. But Sean persists, and Will ramps up his defenses.

With each assurance, the therapist takes a step closer, infringing upon the student's physical and mental space. This continues for the better part of a minute, and just as we can't bear this exchange one more time—the breakthrough happens. Will surrenders his defenses. Sean knows his student has been paralyzed by fear. Will has been believing a lie his world has told him that if he would just cover up his wounds and shoulder the burden alone; he could keep himself from getting hurt anymore. But it took someone he could trust that wouldn't hurt him anymore to break past the walls he had built up to keep himself from feeling. The scene begins with Will as his 'good-humored,' defensive self. It then moves from anger to despair, despair to surrender, surrender to acceptance. He learns the mysterious truth that *"It's NOT OK,"* and at the same time, *"It IS OK."* He submits to the process and allows himself to be changed by it.

In the blink of an eye, it took me discovering and admitting my own unbelief, and everything was different. Heaven had come down to earth and God's love had descended from my lofty mind to penetrate my lowly heart. And it was beautiful. So began the journey of discovery, where God started teaching me all the different ways He designed the heart and mind to interact with each other. The relief that came from this lesson was unimaginable, and it could not have come at a better time.

TRAINING A PUPPY IS ALL about establishing structure, and structure requires a foundation, much like a bond requires two components willing to attach themselves to one another.

Hopefully, it doesn't surprise you to learn that dogs exist in a pack mentality. As domesticated as the species has become, they are still 99 percent wolf. They cannot live any other way. When you bring a dog into your home, you are now a pack, whether you know it or not. And in pack mentality, there is an order that must be observed. I imagine you parents are well familiar with this theory. For you softy dog owners out there (and there's many of you), your sweet, fluffy, four-legged fur ball is in dire need of a pack leader. And if it ain't you, guess who it's going to be? Yep, you called it—Mr. Sniffles will inherently assume that he is the big dog on campus, working toward a master's degree in running your home life.

If you establish yourself as the leader of the pack, the most incredible shift happens. In an attempt to secure its position higher up in the pack order, your dog will innately act out of a desire to please you. Now, this book isn't so much about training techniques (I confess I'm quite the novice compared to the thousands of dog trainers out there). However, I can say with confidence that establishing yourself as the leader is vital to both your sanity and your pup's happiness.

I wonder what our days would look like if we were more in tune with the natural order of our own lives? If we are made in the image of God, then, clearly, we are meant to imitate Him. As a recovering Presbyterian, I tend to think of God only in terms of sovereignty. Among many other characteristics, it's easy for me to forget that Jesus came to serve in the interest of his Father and on behalf of the Love that flowed through Him. This is contrary to the world's take on how we should conduct our lives. At the surface, you would think it's easier just to be your own master, to figure out your own way and answer to no one. But this is the original lie that was told to man, which man chose to believe. There is absolutely zero difference between that lie and the one we are a told a thousand times a day.

The truth is—we aren't equipped for the job of being our master. Still, I try daily.

"How's that been working out for you?" I hear.

"Terribly, God, I've literally tried every single way I can think of to figure out how to do this on my own, but I can't. I'm tired, and I'm hurting. I've hurt so many people, and I feel like a jerk."

This conversation was nothing new. In fact, it was exhaustingly old. But as I continued to be surrounded by God's children, whose hearts were coming alive, I learned an essential question that begins to reveal a beautiful part of God's character.

"How do you feel about the way I've been doing things?" I asked God. You see, we were now entering into a new level of relationship, one that we don't simply speak *at* one another. In this sort of relationship, we actually began to ask each other questions. I'll talk more about this shift in relational dynamic later on, but for now, the conversation went something like this:

"Remember how I told you that you weren't letting my love penetrate to your heart? Well, in order for you to see who I've truly made you to be, you have to allow that love to

permeate into every layer that comes between you and me. I've been wanting to show you these things for years, but until you're ready to go swimming, we're going to stay here. Me in the water and you on the shore. We'll still be together . . . but it could be wildly different."

"This is going to take a while, isn't it?"

"Yep. But there's no rush. We'll take it one step at a time."

And just like that, my *"I can't trust you"* became *"I can't not trust you,"* or, in other words: *"Whatever it looks like, I now want to trust you more than continuing to do things the way I've been doing them."* In short, *"I give up."*

In that particular area of my heart, I learned how to surrender, and that's when God began to transform my perspective of discipline.

"And have you completely forgotten this word of encouragement that addresses you as a father addresses his son? It says, 'My son, do not make light of the Lord's discipline, and do not lose heart when He rebukes you, because the Lord disciplines the one He loves, and chastens everyone He accepts as his son. Endure hardship as discipline; God is treating you as His children. No discipline seems pleasant at the time, but painful. Later on, however, it produces a harvest of righteousness and peace for those who have been trained by it. Therefore, strengthen your feeble arms and weak knees. Make level paths for your feet, so that the lame may not be disabled, but rather healed. You have come to Mount Zion, to the city of the living God, the heavenly Jerusalem. You have come to thousands upon thousands of angels in joyful assembly, to the church of the firstborn, whose names are written in heaven. You have come to God." (Hebrews 12:5-23)

Growing up as I did, in a fundamentalist home, rules ruled everything. I didn't have the wherewithal or the backbone to break the rules—big or small. But things began to shift when I got into high school and the clear lines of my youth began to blur.

I put up a valiant effort, but considering the world to which I was being exposed, it was only a matter of time before I would disregard the rules.

The summer after my freshman year, I was out on my buddy's runabout boat when I got a phone call from my mom. She wasn't thrilled with how I had neglected to mention I was going out on the lake. She instructed me to come home within the hour. I was pissed (in hindsight, I was embarrassed); I was going to show her. Most of my friends had been smoking and using smokeless tobacco for more than a year, and I had successfully managed to fend off the peer pressure. But today was different. I remember thinking, *I'm not a kid anymore*, even though it was one of the more childish reactions I can recall ever having.

That day I decided I'd had enough of the overbearing discipline. It was time to throw the rulebook out the window. I didn't know how monumental that decision was until many years later, when I began to see to what extent that mentality had become the hidden motive behind so many of my life choices. I had to learn the hard way how isolating and damaging that perspective can be. By grace, I was spared from the complete destruction this path often leads people to, though I suffered greatly for it.

I can't think of a better analogy for my skewed perspective of discipline than the railing I ignored on the balcony that day. The railing was intended for my safety; it was put in place for the explicit purpose of allowing me to enjoy the balcony without falling to the rocks below. Like all boundaries, this railing could be broken, and the consequences for doing so were tremendous.

The Thrill of the Hunt

Thankfully, as God's love began to seep into my heart, He revealed the part of me that I'd thrown away with my childhood fifteen years earlier. My tiny, negative view of discipline could only see the punishment; from God's view, it can look quite different. He says that discipline is good for us. He says that instead of punishment, we need to have eyes to see discipline as love.

I'VE NOTICED AN AMUSING PARADOX when it comes to the way we view dog training. If I said that I discipline Yonah multiple times every day, some of you might be alarmed, envisioning me just following him around with a leather belt waiting for him to make a mistake. You might say, *"Rob, don't you think you're being a little tough?"* But if I told you I train Yonah throughout the day, you might say, *"Oh, wow, that's great that you have such discipline."*

Wait, first you say I'm being a little tough, and now you're admiring my persistence? What changed?

I think the biggest difference is in the way we interpret the words 'discipline' and 'training.' Discipline tends to be viewed as reactionary, while training is pre-actionary, (preparatory, if we're being fancy). There's another common misconception of discipline versus training: discipline is usually thought of in terms of a superior reprimanding his inferior, but training suggests two beings working together to achieve a common goal. What enables trainers to carry out each method is their vision for what they *and* their trainees want to achieve.

As sons and daughters, we don't get to decide how and when we get disciplined. Nor does Yonah get to decide how long he's going to be trained. Without constant correction, certain tendencies will become awful habits, ones that will be much more difficult to break the longer they go unchecked.

Some of you don't have to think too hard here, but imagine what your friend would say if every time you brought Mr. Sniffles over for a casual visit, he chewed a new hole in the drywall? Unless your friend is Gandhi reincarnate, I doubt you'd get an invite to your friend's next game night.

Undergoing at least some level of training would be beneficial for both Mr. Sniffles's tummy and the aesthetic integrity of your friend's house, not to mention your relationship with your friend. Again, don't confuse discipline with punishment. What kind of empty relationship would I have with Yonah if I constantly give him the chain and the boot in hopes of getting him to do what I ask? Punishment is only a small portion of discipline, and any thoughtful parent knows reprimand is actually a last resort.

Training starts with a goal. The first step is to help the puppy understand what is being asked of it. The trainer shares a portion of the bigger picture, and—after much patience, *repetition*, and encouragement—the puppy slowly starts to get the idea. By affirmation, the trainer reaches deep beyond the puppy's surface level distractions and strikes a nerve in the dog's innate desire to please its master. This makes encouragement and reward the first tools a good trainer will utilize, reserving punishment as the last straw.

"No discipline seems pleasant at the time, but painful. Later on, however, it produces a harvest of righteousness and peace for those who have been trained by it. Therefore, strengthen your feeble arms and weak knees." (Hebrews 12:11)

Take a moment and think back to a time in your life when a parent or teacher disciplined you. Do you recall your feelings? Were you stubborn, suspicious, and defiant? Or were you trusting and excited at the thought of a new challenge? Well, if you are the latter, then I want to meet you and shake your hand, because you, my friend, are among the few and far between.

Our typical response to any type of discipline is one of immediate defensiveness. We try to justify our present situation, insisting the comfort of now is far more enticing than the promise of the future. Could it be that we have a gross misunderstanding of discipline? What if discipline wasn't synonymous with punishment but was understood more as an invitation to look at something differently, or as the process through which we are transformed by the renewing of our minds? Cast in this light, discipline looks more like adventure than punishment.

Unfortunately I could not yet see it this way, and as the years went on, I became in bondage to my false sense of freedom. There I sat, wondering why I wasn't getting better (whatever that meant). I often wondered if I was diseased or plagued. My despair became so bad at times that I pleaded with God to do whatever was necessary to stop me from feeling this way. "*Whatever it takes.*"

Years went by and I continued to strive for perfection. With every miserably inevitable failure, I became more and more exhausted. I questioned what God was waiting for and why he was taking so long to answer my prayer, never realizing that what I truly longed for was not perfection but true freedom.

Pablo Giacopelli's masterfully insightful book, *Holding on Loosely*, recounts his own journey toward understanding this process of letting go and trusting God:

"We exhaust ourselves by the efforts we make in order to reach the destination where we believe we will finally find God. But God lives on the road of grace, where performance and behavior take a second seat to life, love, and relationship. On this road, we are free to be ourselves. No more manipulations and false pretenses. No more bargaining and forcing. No more religion and rules. Just life.

To God, the condition of our hearts is what matters first. The heart is the place Life originates. The heart is the place where everything in our lives begins. The perfect love that only God can give us is the remedy that all our hearts are seeking. Too many of us have missed this love (and continue to miss it) because we focus on our behavior, trying to be perfect."[1]

What Pablo began to see was that when we face the onset of discipline, we come to a fascinating fork in the road. The choice is quite simple: Don't confuse simplicity with inconsequential. We can choose to submit—to surrender our immediate desires and trust in the promise of a deeper level of satisfaction. Or, we can resist—stay in the shallow waters and hope someone or something more ideal will come along and give us the desires of our heart.

I CAN'T THINK OF A more accurate portrayal of this invitation to adventure than the Wachowski Brothers' film, *The Matrix*. Here we find our protagonist, Neo, in a relentless search, so relentless that the first time we see him, he's passed out in front of his computer after searching all night for an answer to a question. He doesn't even know what he's searching for, but he knows *it* is out there, and whatever *it* is must certainly be more meaningful than his present, dumpy life at a tech company. Neo knows he's stuck in a meaningless existence, and he's willing to search for something better. For the rest of Act I, Neo (which, by the way, means 'New') wrestles with this tension. In some instances, he takes risks. In others, he cowers in fear and digresses to his imprisoned state. And just when we can't bear the ups and downs one more time, he receives an invitation from his mentor, Morpheous (whose name is only too perfect for his role in inciting the potential for growth).

Before lifting the veil from the Matrix, Morpheus offers Neo a choice. Two opposing paths to follow, or symbolically swallow, in the form of two capsules—the blue pill . . . and the red pill.

Morpheus says, "*You take the blue pill, the story ends. You wake up in your bed and believe whatever you want to believe. You take the red pill, you stay in Wonderland, and I show you how deep the rabbit hole goes.*"

The subtext for the scene is perfect, even down to the color of the pills. Blue—representing comfort and safety. Red—implicative of risk and pain. Which pill do you think our protagonist chose to swallow? Of course, he reaches for the red pill! What kind of story would it be if he chose to remain in his insulated, safe, yet empty existence? Fascinatingly enough, Neo begins to trust the process, and the rest of the movie is about uncovering who he truly is. If you haven't seen the movie, I recommend it. If you have, watch it again.

"*That night God appeared to Solomon and said to him, 'Ask for whatever you want me to give you.' [Solomon replied] "Give me wisdom and knowledge, that I may lead this people . . . '*" (2 Chronicles 1:7).

I must have been in high school when I first heard this story of King Solomon's noble request. *That sounds great,* I thought. *I'll have that,* as if I were ordering lunch in the cafeteria line. I asked it, and I meant it, though I had no idea what I was asking for.

Years later, I recalled this prayer and wondered why God had delayed in bestowing me with lofty gifts of wisdom and knowledge. I had earnestly desired to be wise, but my words and my actions consistently spoke of a different desire.

Maybe if I just change my ways, then I'll be considered wise, I thought as I laced up my combat boots.

I admit, after hearing this story, I'd always imagined a young King Solomon lying in bed and making his request to God just before falling asleep. In the morning, he awoke and was happy to discover he was the wisest man on earth. As my life unfolded, I began to doubt this was the case.

I continued to press in to my desire for wisdom and life's reflection of folly, and I developed a strange notion. Now I am *no* theologian, and perhaps true theologians might be tempted to stone me with the same rocks I broke my back on for suggesting this, but what if King Solomon's great wisdom was born out of a lifetime of folly?

Had I misunderstood the text? Had I asked for something far more complex than I could have imagined at the time? And if King Solomon truly was the wisest man to have lived, why on earth would he muse in his old age, "*For with much wisdom comes much sorrow; the more knowledge the more grief?*" (Ecclesiastes 1:18)

It seems to me that the wisest man on earth would have some clue about how to avoid the pain and suffering attributed to our humanity.

As we explore in the next chapter of what training looks like, keep in mind there is no perfect formula for training. When we train, we are training for excellence—not perfection—and no one can tell you what is truly excellent except for the trainer. The relationship between the puppy and the trainer is a fascinating one, as no two puppies are the same. But one thing I have learned about our Master is that He alone *is* the same, and whatever He is to me does not mean that He should be that to you.

We have such limited sight, and if we view our trainer, our Master, through some fixed perspective we have of Him, that's unfortunately all we can allow Him to be in our lives. If we hold on so tightly to that perspective, we ignore the infinite opportunities that God desires to reveal in our lives.

We each have unique gifts, many of which are buried so deeply within the layers of our hearts that only the Master can see them. But rest assured He *does* see them, and He longs for us to see them, too. Paul had wonderful words of encouragement to the church he planted in Philippi about the training process:

"Being confident of this, that He who began a good work in you will carry it on to completion until the day of Jesus Christ." (Philippians 1:6)

What a relief it is that we don't have to carry that burden; instead, we only need to let go and trust in the process of discovery. When we train our puppies or raise our children, we are kidding ourselves if we can't admit that we, too, need training. Our perspectives are far too limited, and our motives are often selfish. Isn't it amazing we serve a Master whose motives are pure and whose sight is infinite? This insight changes everything, and the best part is that it's barely the beginning.

I'm grateful to have you here with me. Even more so, I pray the elementary insights I've been given in this time will spark in you a curiosity to explore what's happening in *your* own life.

Keep in mind that it's entirely OK if you're not ready to start your training process. Maybe you don't see how all this is possible. Maybe you don't believe (as I struggled with for so many years) that God is a good God. Maybe you're still waiting for a sign. Whatever it is, please know that it's OK to be cautious. I encourage you to simply go to your heart about it.

Honesty is a key element in all of this, and I pray you'll be honest with yourself. When you're honest at a heart level, you find a God who has been so eager for you to meet him there. He has so many wonderful things to share with you about who you are. As Paul reminds us, when you are honest at a heart level . . .

. . . *"You have come to Mount Zion, to the city of the living God, the heavenly Jerusalem. You have come to thousands upon thousands of angels in joyful assembly, to the church of the firstborn, whose names are written in heaven. You have come to God."* (Hebrews 12:23)

3

Training

"For everyone who asks receives; the one who seeks finds; and to the one who knocks, the door will be opened to him. Which of you, if your son asks for bread, will give him a stone? Or if he asks for a fish, will give him a snake? If you, then, though you are evil, know how to give good gifts to your children, how much more will your Father in heaven give good gifts to those who ask him!"

—Matthew 7:8-11

DURING OUR FIRST YEAR TOGETHER, I would let Yonah roam free about the farm. Especially as I was recovering from my injuries, I rarely had the energy to take him on long-enough walks to expend his energy.

The training that we had done up to that point was slowly wearing off. Picture a twenty-eight-year-old guy with an eighty-eight-year-old back and an eight-month-old puppy endlessly running circles, figure eights, and all sorts of other abstract geometric shapes around him. Yeah, that was me, and in a last-ditch effort before admitting I needed help, I resolved to let Yonah roam free for a couple hours a day. After all, he *is* a country dog.

At first, I'd let him out and he'd come back an hour later tired, hungry, and happy. It gave me such joy to think about him exploring at will and learning to use his senses. But an hour or so quickly turned into a couple hours, and a couple hours quickly turned into an entire morning.

The last time I let him roam without supervision, he came home five hours later to a nauseatingly worried dad ... with a neighbor's chicken in his mouth. He was so proud of his first kill. I, on the other hand, was appalled. I know two things about bird dogs and chickens. First, once a bird dog strikes up a likin' to killin' chickens, it's damn near impossible to turn them off the easy game. Second, around these parts, killing a neighbor's chicken is the sort of thing that gets a country dog shot.

I had been debating e-collar training for months and decided it was time to raise the white flag. If you're not familiar with an e-collar, it's not so much an electric fence as it is an invisible leash (which I suppose is the same thing as a mobile electric fence). The e-collar receiver goes around Yonah's neck, just like ... well, a collar. And the transmitter is a small handheld device.

Again, just like a crate, an e-collar is not a tool for punishment. If your pup does something wrong, you don't send him, like you would a child, to sit alone in the corner. Even if your dog could understand the concept of 'timeout,' the crate is intended to be the dog's safe place—its den. The same is true for the e-collar. Its intention is to enable the owner to communicate both verbally and physically with the dog at great distances. It's a tool to allow liberty while still maintaining control for the dog's protection.

I know you might be thinking—aren't liberty and control rather contradictory? Well, it turns out they're not, and you might be as relieved as I was to learn why.

Before you go blow a couple hundred bucks on an e-collar, let me be clear in telling you that this is not an easy, quick fix. E-collar training still takes patience, persistence,

Yonah was not nearly as amused as my nephew. In his defense, he didn't fully understand the concept of a seesaw.

and a good bit of reason. If used properly, it's an incredible platform that enables me to let Yonah know I'm always near, admiring his youthful wonderment and looking out for potential dangers. Needless to say, it has opened up a whole new world of adventure for the both of us.

ONE OF THE FIRST THINGS we learn when training a dog is to use simple, one-word commands. If I want Yonah to go sit on his bed (or a seesaw) and not move until I say so, I'm not going to say, "Listen, bud, will you please go over to your bed and stay there until I decide to ask you to do something else?" If I said that, he would likely cock his head and look at me as if I'm an idiot, which he does (quite accurately) more often than I'm comfortable with.

No, if I want him to obey that command, because we've taken the time to establish that 'Place' means 'Go over there and don't move,' I simply point to the object I want him to stay on and say, "Yonah, place."

It took me a long time to learn that God communicates much the same way. I was always looking for Him to reveal some elaborate plan, where I know all the twists and turns and outcomes, enabling me to step forward in confidence. No, our God is far too good of a Father to give us complex commands. If He did that, we would never learn to trust Him. In fact, we would have no need to trust Him. By giving us simple commands or, rather, invitations, He teaches us to trust, and learning to trust God is far more important than any end goal we think we need.

For example, God would never say, *"Listen, Rob, I want you to master dog training and research all there is to know about writing a book. After that, I want you to write a book, and I will show you my favor."* If He did that, I might learn how to write a grammatically perfect book on dog training. But the book itself would be flavorless. It would have no account of the mistakes I've made training my dog, or the thousands of other failures I've had learning what it means to be a child of God.

Instead of that complex, nearly impossible command, He starts by teaching me something much more fundamental. He says, *"Son, I love you,"* which is imperative for me to grasp if I'm to follow any sequential commands well. After that, He might whisper some invitation like, *"Step out,"* which I would interpret as, *"Hey, I've put this desire in your heart to write this book. You don't have to be an expert; just start writing and I'll guide you."* By His speaking in simple, easy-to-comprehend cues, I learn to trust. I learn to move even if I don't see the big picture. He encourages me to press on, even when a task might seem daunting. All I have to do is obey the previous command until He instructs me further.

I'll never forget the first time I was introduced to the e-collar training method. I was at a local beer garden when a girl walked in with an adorable GSP pup. Naturally, I was compelled to introduce myself. As is common when you see someone with a similar breed, you have plenty to talk about, and I related how I grew up with two GSPs and was planning to get another one soon. While we were talking, the young pup was busy sniffing around our feet, and I could tell both the pup and the owner were getting anxious. All of a sudden, in the middle of the owner's sentence, the pup laid down at her feet. I was amazed.

"You just used ESP on your GSP! How in the world did you do that?" I exclaimed.

That's when she humbly opened her palm, revealing the transmitter she'd been holding the whole time.

"No, we're in the middle of e-collar training," she answered as I tried to wipe the look of amazement from my face. She went on to explain that the whole time we were talking, she was giving commands to her pup using the transmitter, and her pup wasn't responding the way she instructed her to, so she delivered a 'stem,' which the pup knew meant it was time to lie down and chill out. We talked a bit longer and I eagerly wrote down the contact information she gave me for the training program.

Fast forward a year later, when Yonah and I began utilizing the e-collar in our training. It opened up a whole new dynamic to our relationship. At first, I used the leash and the e-collar, but as I learned how to effectively communicate with the transmitter, we said goodbye to the leash and hello to the world of controlled liberty.

The e-collar can be used in nearly any situation, though we don't typically use it when we're out at the house. The number of potential dangers is low, and there aren't as many distractions as the city. Unless we sneak up on a deer, Yonah minds well enough. The opposite can be said of a crowded patio or farmers market, and we try to steer clear of those scenarios as best we can. When we do find ourselves in this sort of situation, I'll usually break out the leash just to keep our anxiety levels down.

The e-collar is really best used taking a stroll through a not-so-busy downtown or at the park. When we walk down the sidewalk off-leash, I'll give him the 'heel' command, and he knows to come up to my left side and keep his head between my stride—not one step in front; not one step behind. That way he can always look up at me and observe my body language. Both dogs and humans use an incredibly extensive vocabulary of body language. I try to be as aware as possible of the way I'm communicating to any dog I happen to be around, as well as the people around me.

I catch myself dreaming of the day when we can walk around town with little or no verbal communication, but Yonah is still young, and we still have a lot of training to do. His nose is very active and there are plenty of distractions, so the 'heel' command is a constant. There are a couple of smaller parks downtown, where we often find squirrels and sparrows scrounging around looking for lunch. When walking to and from these parks, I always keep Yonah at my side. But when we get to the hunting fields of Krutch Park, I loosen the reins and watch him go to work. Watching any work dog do its job is a treat, but I'm partial to bird dogs and their intense focus and patience. It's admirable and fascinating on so many levels. Since Yonah is a work dog by breed and a pet by choice, it's a funny mixture of awesome and awkward.

I've seen countless groups of passersby stop dead in their tracks and watch him sneak up on an unknowing squirrel. As Yonah crouches low and stealthily approaches, he innately stops about a half-dozen yards away. The tension of this moment is incredible, and even more impressive is that we didn't spend one second training for this exercise. This is all instinct; he couldn't change it if he (or I) wanted him to. You can see his nose going wild, but the rest of his body is tensely frozen. In a split second, he takes off and flushes the terrified squirrel up the nearest tree. Yonah doesn't always see the squirrel scatter up the backside of the tree and sometimes he'll start combing the park for any remaining scent. That's when I whistle him off, and he circles back to come happily sit beside his master who's now beaming with pride.

In moments like this, I like to imagine Yonah is constantly aware of my presence. But in reality, I'm the last thing on his mind when there's a furry or feathery critter around. He unknowingly depends on me in these moments to keep him safe. There's been plenty of times Yonah has locked up on a bird across the street. Replay the previous scenario outside the park and across a busy street. Yeah, it doesn't end up the same way, and the only thing that keeps that from happening is me, his master. I am aware of his surroundings even when, rather *especially* when, he is not. We'll talk more about this higher perspective in the next chapter, but, for now, let's remain present and talk about staying in the present moment.

As humans, we're constantly (yet subconsciously) aware of our mortality. One might think the logical thing to do would be to enjoy every second of our life. In truth, we tend to do the exact opposite, always reliving past events or trying to prepare for whatever we think the future will present. More often than not, we find that our actions in the present moment are directed by these unseen motivators.

We think of the past, *Oh, if I would have just done this or that differently, then I would definitely feel better about that situation.*

47

Or maybe we look ahead to some future event and think, *All right, all I have to do is A, B, and C, and voila! Then I'll be golden.*

But we deceive ourselves.

Similar to the way Yonah obsesses over every critter that catches his attention, we become fixated on our desires and shortcomings; we assume control and place an expectation on ourselves or on a specific outcome. In doing so, we sabotage our efforts and slip away to a place of even less control—either the past or the future.

We spend a third of our entire lives asleep, but I wonder what portion of our waking lives we spend sleep-walking through our days, constantly dreaming about some elusive event. What a tragedy!

So where can we trace this broken perspective back to its source? Well, in Pablo's second book, *The Modern Fig Leaf*, he explores the incident in the Garden of Eden. That's when Adam and Eve made a simple yet unknowing choice to look after themselves instead of trusting that God would provide their every need and desire. As a result of their decision, they suddenly became shamefully aware of their nakedness, subsequently causing the rest of mankind to spend its days attempting to hide their shame by covering themselves with various forms of modern fig leaves.

In the first and forever best moment of foreshadowing, God slays a lamb and covers them with the animal's flesh. After clothing them, God begins to explain the consequences of their decision to come under the curse of sin. God essentially says, "This is how it's going to be for a while (at least until I step in and rewrite the playbook)." In Pablo's words, God turns to Eve and says—

"'Eve, for all underlying premises you need to live a healthy and whole life; you are now going to turn and look to

your husband to deliver them to you. This is because you came from Adam and he is what is in closest proximity to you.' And to Adam he said, 'Adam, all the underlying premises you need to live a healthy and whole life, you are now going to turn and look to the ground to deliver them to you. This again is because you came from the ground, and so this is what is in closest proximity to you.' And so Eve turns to Adam and demands these things from him, and Adam replies, 'I am not God.' Adam equally turns to the ground and demands these things from it, and the ground replies, 'I am not God.'" [1]

PABLO GOES INTO GREAT DEPTH in his discovery of the various ways these modern fig leaves manifest themselves in our lives, including, but certainly not limited to, religion. He does an incredible job of exploring these labels from every angle, and I implore you to get your hands on both of Pablo's books. They were extremely instrumental in my waking up to life, and I'm certain they would do the same for you.

I only share this insight because I have discovered how imperative it is to observe and understand the core motivations behind our actions. If we become aware of these motives buried deep beneath the layers of our consciousness, we find ourselves in a space where we can simply observe and talk to God about them. Miraculously, the impossible, burdensome task of having to manipulate the world for affirmation simply falls away.

As I began to talk to God about what He was showing me, I kept getting hung up on this word 'turn.' The Bible says that Eve *turned* to Adam and Adam *turned* to the ground. *Turned* meaning—stayed where they were but changed what they were looking at (and for). I wonder what would it look like to *turn* back and see, with confidence, that we are in perfect stride with our Master?

The Thrill of the Hunt

Everyone has his or her own opinion about the morality of an e-collar. Some are shocked at the thought of shocking their dog in order to achieve a specific result; others follow their dog around like Zeus on a cloud raining down thunderous bolts of lightning every time their dog looks at them the wrong way. It's always funny to hear how different people feel about the concept, and they certainly don't mind telling you.

I always explain that now we've established a structure with the training, Yonah ultimately gets to decide how it's going to go, according to his level of cooperation. It's an agreement we've made in order to go to the places we want to go to and not have to drag each other around with a leash. When the e-collar is on, there's really only one way—my way—because it's my responsibility to keep him safe, and I have to be able to trust him to obey. That doesn't mean he has to sit at my side moping because he can't go play. He's free to roam at will as long as he stays where I can see him and he minds when I communicate to him. In order to enjoy the freedom of life off-leash, he has to remember our agreement. I have to know his tendencies and be able to see potential dangers that he doesn't have the sense to see. My job is to look out for him; his job is to be a dog and spread joy and happiness to all the little children.

Let's say, for example, we're hanging out on the patio at one of our favorite breweries. I'm sitting there with a nice cold beer in my hand and going on with the talented fellows who have crafted this nice cold beer I'm enjoying. Yonah's off sniffing around and making some little kid's day, and I glance around making sure we're all good. I hear a little girl giggling and smile to find Yonah prancing around her by the sidewalk. (He takes on a different energy around little kids, and he gets really happy whenever he has their attention.) Out of the corner of my eye, I see a couple heading down the

Just to give a contextual location for this hypothetical situation, as described in the surrounding text.

sidewalk on their bikes. It's a nice day, the sun is out, and everybody has the right to safe passage on the sidewalk. Yonah doesn't know that common courtesy, and I can see his excitement for the little girl is ramping up.

Knowing this could get ugly, I simply reach down to the transmitter hanging from my belt loop and deliver a quick 'chirp.' Yonah perks up, remembers our agreement, and prances back to take a seat beside me. The bikers pass, unaware that Yonah's playfulness could have quickly taken the joy out of their joyride.

Thankfully, in that hypothetical scenario, Yonah chose to adhere to the 'chirp' and the bikers went on to ride another day. But the 'chirp' is only one of the functions of the e-collar. In a less-urgent situation, I always give Yonah one or two verbal commands and an opportunity to respond. If he chooses to ignore that, then he gets the 'chirp,' which is roughly the equivalent of reaching for the door knob and getting a pulse of static electricity through your hand. It doesn't exactly hurt, and the pulse is really just a reinforcement of the 'chirp' that Yonah hears from the receiver next to his ear. It essentially serves as a reminder, *Oh, yeah, Dad's watching.*

Yonah's a pretty smart, submissive pup, and it doesn't take much to get his attention. But every once in a while, a distraction comes along, a subject so enticing that he's willing to forgo the consequences and completely disregard our agreement. That's when the 'chirp' becomes the 'lightning rod,' and the duration and intensity of the thunderstorm is entirely determined by Yonah.

In this circumstance, there is a magic number on a scale of 0-100 at which Yonah will abandon his short-sighted goal in favor of doing what Dad is asking him to do. Whatever distraction seemed so irresistible is suddenly not so imperative. Since I'm the master, I get to decide what *we* are going to do. But the level of discomfort associated with this discipline is solely up to Yonah.

DURING OUR TRAINING WITH THE e-collar, I'm often reminded how God communicates His intentions for us much in the same way. Thankfully, we don't have to wear a collar around our neck and receive an electric shock in order to receive his instructions (though many of us would probably benefit from that sort of obvious signal). Instead, He uses a different platform to communicate His love for us. And it's a platform we're well versed in.

In C. S. Lewis's *The Problem of Pain,* the author makes the fascinating suggestion that "Pain insists upon being attended to. God whispers to us in our pleasures, speaks in our consciences, but shouts in our pains. It is his megaphone to rouse a deaf world."

I read this years ago and remember being dumbfounded at its profundity. If pain insists on being attended to, then what exactly is it saying? Well, first, let's imagine a world without pain. I don't mean in the heavenly sense, where God will wipe away every tear and pain, death, and sadness will be no more. I mean, imagine living in the same broken world we find ourselves presently, yet not being able to feel physical pain. It would be a disaster!

Think about the first caveman who discovered fire after lightning struck down a tree next to his cave. Surely, he reached out and touched this mysterious light source, quickly finding that it's much more pleasurable to admire from a distance rather than by touch. Without pain, he would have grabbed the log and turned around to show his caveman buddies, realizing his fingers were melting off and his new nickname was 'Knubby.' Instead, by the law of evolution, his brain received the pain memo and did what it was designed to do—adapt to the situation. He was forced to come up with a creative solution to enjoy the many benefits of fire without losing his digits.

I don't think C. S. Lewis was thinking of Knubby when he stumbled onto this mysterious problem of pain. And assuming we all agree that pain has its place in our world, why is it that we work so relentlessly to avoid it? I wonder how else we could direct our energies, knowing that pain is inevitable.

Next, what can we learn from his observation: "God whispers to us in our pleasures, speaks to us in our consciences, but shouts in our pains. It is his megaphone to rouse a deaf world"?

Well right off the bat, I think the statement begs the question—What is so important to God that He persists across these platforms instead of dropping the mic and leaving us to fend for ourselves?

I think we'd all agree that pleasure is a good thing. If an all-loving God is whispering through it, we have to imagine He is gently affirming His love for us and reminding us of His presence. If I'm sitting on my porch enjoying a peaceful afternoon, and I come to the realization of how much I like moments like this, God does not need to fire a shotgun over my head to get my attention. He already has it, and He both made me to enjoy the moment and made the moment for me to enjoy.

Instead of the shotgun approach, He will simply whisper, *"Rob, you know that I love you, right?"*

To which I might respond by saying, *"Yes, God, I know that you love me. Thank you for giving me this wonderful moment that I can just be alive with you and able to enjoy the little things in life like a nice autumn day, porches in general, and, of course, this frothy beverage in my hand that makes me feel warm and fuzzy. You are a good, good Father; thank you for reminding me."*

Yes, God often speaks His love to us in our pleasurable moments. But, surprisingly, this comes from a great deal of training or practice. That same peaceful moment on the porch would have gone much differently if the chatter in my mind blocked the message of love that was intended for my heart. Without training, it's here that I would have entered into the conscience and responded in a number of unpleasant ways.

Even if I heard God whisper the same thing, *"Rob, you know that I love you, right?"* I might be full of self-pity and say, *"Oh, yeah, God, if you love me, then why the @#$% did _____ happen?"* I'd essentially be saying, *"If you're really God and you say that you love me, then why didn't you stop that from happening so I wouldn't have to feel like this right now?"* That conversation would continue aimlessly until I realized that my glass is empty, and I've got five more beers in the fridge. At that point, I would walk inside and begin numbing my discomfort for the rest of the afternoon. I could avoid that conversation (and I did) for years without making a single stride to relieve my discomfort. And perhaps the most amazing thing about this postponement is that, *because* of those years, I was finally brought to a place (of immense pain) where I could no longer run, and I *turned* to face the issue instead of eluding it.

It was and is *because* of those years of training that I've now learned to hear God's voice through the megaphone of pain. I know firsthand how futile it is to avoid what's being said and quickly remember how much easier it is to simply turn and face it. Surprisingly, when I turn and face it, I again hear God speaking gently in my conscience. As I submit to what He is saying, my being is soothed by the sound of His loving whisper that resounds in my heart.

I'm very much still learning this practice, but I'm able to enjoy moments like this much more frequently. I'm grateful that God loves me enough to bust out his megaphone and rouse my numbingly deaf self to life. And, much like Yonah, I often get to choose how high the volume knob on that megaphone is turned up.

Coming from someone who was nearly deafened by the megaphone itself, don't think for a minute that volume knob caps out at 100. Don't think for a second that there is a place you can run to where God will stop pursuing your heart and speaking His love for you. If you so choose, God will yell His love through a megaphone of pain for the rest of your life, but He would prefer that you listen to your tears and hear His whisper of love.

JESUS REPLIED, *"A time is coming and in fact has come when you will be scattered, each to your own home. You will leave me all alone. Yet I am not alone, for my Father is with me. I have told you these things, so that in me you may have peace. In this world, you will have trouble. But take heart! I have overcome the world."* (John 16:32-33)

Jesus spoke these words only hours before the unimaginably painful weight of the entire world's sin was placed on His shoulders. He knew the pain was coming; He knew it was the only way. Moments later, His closest friends abandoned Him at the first sign of trouble. Out of fear, they scattered. They might have cognitively believed He was who He said He was, but they didn't yet believe it in their hearts. Like many of us, they didn't yet realize that Jesus came to address the very fear that scatters us all to the homes we build to shelter us from the pain we can't avoid. Jesus came to abolish that fear by placing His home in our hearts. And if His home is in our hearts, then we share in His glory—the glory He had with the Father before the world began.

Some of us need to take heart today. We know that pleasure and pain are a reality in this present darkness, but if we learn to see them as a platform of conversation that exists within our hearts, we find that we are invited to respond. In this world, pain will never be completely removed from the picture, though we can forever learn to live in a way that pain (or the avoidance of it) doesn't control our every thought and action.

What are the various faces of pain in your own life? What would it look like to stare at it objectively—without remorse or repugnance—and allow it to simply exist in your present moment? Can you hear your Father in that space? And if so, what is He saying?

I had to break my back in order for me to hear God whisper His love; in order for me to take heart and believe that Jesus overcame the world long before I set foot in it. But if my back has to ache for the rest of my life so that my heart can become free, now that sounds like the adventure of a lifetime filled with trials and perils, victories and losses. When once I only wanted to live the 'happily ever after' part of the story, I now want to experience every part of the adventure, all because I'm learning to embrace the pain. It's not easy, but it's real, and God cares more about honesty than comfort.

This discomfort reminds me of what has taken place. The pain echoes across the vast distance my Master was willing to go in search of me. It unveils the various levels of pain the people around me are experiencing at any given moment. God is miraculously healing my heart while simultaneously breaking it for my brothers and sisters beside me. He has given me eyes to see their pain and ears to hear all their hopes and fears. I watch the way we interact with each other, acting out of the wounds we have each suffered. I want to reach out and hug them. I want to tell them how much Jesus loves them, but all I can do is listen, ask questions, and silently pray for God to bring them to a place where they can see His love firsthand.

There's a great big world out there, and, like Yonah, I need to trust my Master. My Master knows what I need, and He takes great joy in giving those things to me. When I'm out running in the field with my ears flopping in the wind, I know that my Master is watching over me with a great big smile and a heart filled with joy that I'm doing what I was made to do. Like Yonah's e-collar, training can be confusing and painful, but it can bring us to a new level of freedom, where we don't need to know the outcome in order to enjoy the adventure of the day. This freedom came because my Master shared glimpses of the bigger picture and invited me to follow one step at a time.

Top photo: Yonah in front of kayak.
Bottom photo: Yonah seated in foggy water.

4

Bird's Eye View

"Jesus sat in the midst of joy sipping the coming sorrow, so we can sit in the midst of sorrow and sip the coming joy."

— Timothy Keller, author and theologian

"For my thoughts are not your thoughts, neither are your ways my ways," declares the Lord. "As the heavens are higher than the earth, so are my ways higher than your ways and my thoughts than your thoughts."

— Isaiah 55:8-9

FOR MONTHS, EVERY TIME I REVEALED THE E-COLLAR, Yonah would drop his head, lower his ears, and reluctantly mope over to my feet. Because he is more human than dog, he would say something along the lines of *"Really? I thought we were past this. How about we skip the collar from now on and go straight to the trust part?"*

"Nice try, buddy. Remember last time? Maybe when you're older." I'd reply.

The truth is—he doesn't remember the last time. But I do, and every time I forget, it continually reminds me that he is still very much a puppy. Recall the beer garden/biker scenario from the last chapter? Yonah didn't disregard the two bikers because he's not into third wheeling. Yonah disregarded the bikers because he's a puppy and there was a three-year-old-girl who was infatuated with him (and vice

59

versa). I was able to prevent that hypothetical situation because I was looking ahead. I saw Yonah. I saw the little girl. I saw the bikers. I took into account all the variables involved and, because I know his tendencies better than he does, I realized I needed to intervene before the bikers' unbeknownst fork in the road became a fork in Yonah's shoulder blades. I was able to prevent that situation because I was able to see the bigger picture.

I know all of Yonah's tendencies because I'm his master. Yonah doesn't even know what a tendency is. His capacity to foresee extends about as far as the reach of his nose, which is great for bird hunting and not so great for developing practical life lessons. As far as he's concerned, the scent in his nose at any given moment is everything the world has to offer.

When we're out walking in the pasture, he's not thinking about when he's going to eat dinner. His only concern is to discover where that curious scent in his nose is coming from and what in the world it is. I also know that when he finds it, it's either going to take flight or scurry up the nearest tree, after which Yonah will prance around perplexed that this creature would prefer to play alone up in some distant tree rather than stick around and be his friend. (He's such a sweet dog and truly wants to play with everything that moves. Imagine the countless birds and critters that have missed out on a vibrant friendship with Yonah simply because they think he wants to turn them into a meal.)

But he doesn't regret this rejection too long. He immediately moves on in search of the next scent. As I've watched this interaction endlessly repeat itself, I'm learning that, for Yonah, life is about the thrill of the hunt, and I wonder if we are not so different. But because he's so intent on satisfying this primitive urge, he often loses his awareness that the world is much larger than the scent in his nose.

He doesn't understand the very real dangers surrounding him. He's oblivious to the cars racing down the road. He has no recollection of the time he killed a neighbor's chicken, and he certainly doesn't have the awareness that the neighbor threatened to shoot him next time he did so. We lived out in the sticks, meaning there were plenty of good ol' boys that wouldn't mind a nice stud like Yonah to breed with their inbred beagles. There are poisonous snakes in the nooks and crannies of the streams in which Yonah loves to splash around, and river currents that are too deep and fast for even the best of human swimmers. All of these things are very clear and present dangers in Yonah's life. He can't see any of them, and without my ability to foresee potential dangers and steer him away, the thrill of the hunt can quickly turn into a disaster.

REMEMBER EARLIER WHEN WE DISCUSSED how my stepping out into the world resembled a child squirming out of his parents' arms to go play with some fascinating toy? And after playing with that toy for a while, I would eventually lose interest and move on to the next? When I began to talk about that tendency I have to go in search of something other than His love, I wondered what God was feeling in those moments. I presumed He was disappointed that I didn't want to stay in His embrace.

I imagined Him saying, *"Rob, you know that those things cannot give you the love that you seek. Why do you repeatedly insist on going after them?"*

But then I realized that presumption was coming out of a place of shame, and we know that shame is never from God. What, then, was He feeling? Or rather, what was He saying to me in those moments of inevitable pain and emptiness that come from seeking life from a dead world?

"*The truth is, Rob, you* don't *know that those things cannot give you the love that you seek. I know it, but you don't, and if I stopped you every time you repeatedly insisted on going after them, you would have begun to resent me, believing that I was somehow holding out on you. But because of my love for you and because I'm able to see things from an infinitely higher perspective, I allowed you to go after them knowing that you would eventually learn only I can give you the love that you seek. It's at that point that you would choose to remain in my embrace rather than me holding you against your will.*"

"*God, you really love me that much that you would let me run away from you, knowing how much pain I would cause myself and those around me?*"

"*I really do, child, and so much more. Your desire to seek the fullness of life wasn't a bad thing. In fact, I placed that desire within you. You were just seeking life in the wrong places, Rob. Now you know firsthand that only I can give you that love you seek. You're also beginning to see that you could never truly step out of my embrace. So, I'm going to use your desire to seek the fullness of life, and through it I'm going to show you how much I truly love you. And then you are going to share that love with your brothers and your sisters.*"

"*Wow, that sounds like an adventure!*"

"*You have no idea.*"

ONE OF MY FAVORITE THINGS about dogs is how they inspire us to live in the fullness of every moment. Because they are so grounded in the now, their minds aren't capable of manipulating the present moment in order to achieve some desired outcome. It's true that we, as humans, have an incredible gift of the mind; we are able to analyze, calculate, learn, and prepare. But the mind is a double-edged sword.

It can be more hurtful than helpful if we don't learn the limits of this weapon and begin to wield it properly.

Like dogs, we, too, are bound to the present, but our human minds grant us the freedom to choose to live in the present or to wander outside it. Unfortunately, if we're honest with ourselves, we rarely make the right decision. Our minds have the capacity to perceive images of events that have already taken place as well as visions that we project into our future. We view these recollections and projections through a very small window. Our perception of them is blurry at best. Because we always fear what we don't know, we both consciously and unconsciously try to manipulate the now. When we live from our minds, our lives are about control— a dangerous illusion.

God not only gave us the incredible gift of the mind but also the gift of the present, and He designed us to dwell here. What got us in trouble was when Adam and Eve (who represent us) chose to believe that God was holding out on them and decided to take matters into their own hands. What they failed to realize, or believe, is that the Garden already offered them everything they could ever want. Humanity already dwelt within the fullness of God, and there was literally nothing else for us that we didn't already have.

If we paraphrase Genesis 2, we see that God had been fully transparent with them: *"Look about the Garden. I have made all this for you to enjoy, and I have set you over all of creation. I designed you to live within the structure of our relationship, so don't leave here. It's not good for you to be elsewhere."*

When Adam chose to disregard that natural design for his relationship with God, he unknowingly stepped out of the Garden and entered into this present darkness by coming under the law. And while the world works tirelessly to disprove God's existence and Love for His creation, God uttered a Word to all of creation long before time began—an eternal invitation for us to live with Him in the Garden. When that Word became flesh and dwelt among us, Jesus, too, chose to leave the Garden, and even stepped out of His Kingdom when He offered himself up on the cross for us.

Jesus's victory over death proved that He alone has the power to come and go freely from the Garden, and that power removes our banishment from the Garden! What really blows my mind is that when Jesus appeared to Mary Magdalene for the first time after His glorious resurrection, she met Him in a garden and presumed Him to be the gardener . . . and He was *the* Gardener—*the* Gardener who draws forth life from the ground. We found ourselves banished from the Garden because of our sin (the opposite of love), and it's also in a garden that we learned our banishment had been lifted by, and because of, God's Love.

My friends, we serve a God who loves to lavish us with gifts of His infinite love and glory. He loves to reveal glimpses of His mystery. While the day has not yet come when we can forever return to live in the Garden, we do, by grace, occasionally find ourselves within a vision of the Garden. I encourage you to bask and revel in those visions. I can assure you that is the most alive we will ever be in this brief in-between-life that we find ourselves in at present.

We can't dwell within His peace when we wrestle with doubts and fears that often enter our limited perspective, but when we rest in the original structure of our relationship with God, we find that we know everything we need to know in order to be fully alive and rooted in the present moment. Our trust in God opens us to the beautiful mystery of Life all around us. I take great pleasure in exploring this mystery without the need to see the bigger picture or to somehow solve the riddle and prove it to be right or wrong.

I encourage you to do the same with the glimpses of mystery He shares with you. But let's be careful not to obsess over the mystery because that, too, would be a form of control. Instead, hold it loosely in the light of God's love. Examine it from different angles. Thank Him for sharing it with you and ask Him any questions that arise. Ask him to speak to your heart about it, then simply set it down and walk away. Trust that in His time, He will begin to train your eyes and ears to receive the insights that will help you fulfill the purpose for which you were created.

I WAS NEVER VERY GOOD at reading the Bible while growing up. With my family's weekly regimen of church and Bible studies, in addition to the Christian school I attended, I was quite familiar with virtually all of the stories. I've never read the Bible from start to finish, and the details might, now, get a little blurry toward the latter prophets. But by the time I was fourteen, I at least knew the historical lineage from start to finish.

The reason I was not very good at it was because I was always trying to insert myself into the story. It's a habit which, I later found out, formed some lofty expectations for myself. The tragic part about this behavior is that it completely obscures the point of every single story in the pages. Because of the human condition, we perceive ourselves as the main character of every story, especially our own. Therefore, we give ourselves very little grace because we believe the happy ending we're all expecting depends entirely upon our own actions.

What inconceivable pressure we put on ourselves! What a tremendous life we miss if we're looking at it through the peephole in our front door! Thankfully, God adds a whole cast of characters to spice up our lives and bring new perspective. And if we allow Him to do so, God goes to work tearing down walls we build between us in order to welcome us into the great big world He's made for us to enjoy together. But let's not forget we were primarily made for God's pleasure, not the other way around. Sound selfish? It sounds like grace to me.

Thomas Merton, the great twentieth-century mystic, puts it like this:

"What is 'grace'? It is God's own life, shared by us. God's life is Love. By grace we are able to share in the infinitely selfless love of Him Who is such pure actuality that He needs nothing and therefore cannot conceivably exploit anything for selfish ends. Indeed, outside of Him is nothing, and whatever exists, exists by His free gift of its being, so that one of the notions that is absolutely contradictory to the perfection of God is selfishness. It is metaphysically impossible for God to be selfish, because the existence of everything that is depends upon His gift, depends upon His unselfishness." [1]

Grace can often be easily missed, which is why God takes great joy in giving us new eyes to see grace all around us. This is the 'renewal of the mind' Paul talks about in Romans 12. We opened our discussion reveling in King David's prose about the intricacies of our humanity. We'll circle back around to that discussion in a later chapter, but in order to properly admire King David (the man whose lineage God chose to enter the world through) we must also examine his predecessor, King Saul. Saul was the first anointed King of Israel, after the Israelites complained that they wanted to be like other nations and have a king instead of being led solely by God—a lesson, perhaps, for another time.

The Israelites were always getting picked on like the puny kid at school. They comprised the smallest nation around, and God's delivering them out of Egypt and into the Promised Land just so happened to bring them into an incredibly fertile stretch of land that surrounding nations wanted for themselves with a desire to turn the Israelites back into slaves. Because of this, the nation of Israel was constantly under invasion, especially by their neighbors, the Philistines.

King Saul was famous for his rash decision-making, and his son, Jonathan, was always suffering for it. In fact, it ended up costing both their lives. Jonathan and his men had recently defeated a garrison of Philistines and killed a governor near a city called Gibeah. In Saul's 'infinite' wisdom, he sent a decree to the Hebrews, saying that he, personally, had killed the governor and defeated the Philistines. Unfortunately, when you start bragging about a victory before it's a victory, it tends to anger your enemy and give them plenty of incentive to rally their own troops. Saul meant it as a rallying cry for the men of Israel to join his army at Gilgal. The Philistines, however, hacked his email and discovered his plans. They sent their own troops into and around the mountain village of Micmash, about seven miles north of Jerusalem. They had three companies of chariots (a chariot is the equivalent of a modern-day tank) and enough infantrymen said to have numbered the sands of the seashore.

When the Israelites realized they were in trouble, many hid in caves and among the rocks, while others crossed the fords of the Jordan River with their tails between their legs. Saul and the few thousand men who remained with him at Gilgal trembled as the shadow of the enemy loomed over them.

Samuel, one of the many judges that God used to lead His people, had instructed Saul to wait at Gilgal for seven days. When Samuel didn't show up, Saul's numbers dwindled with each passing day as the people scattered in fear. Again, Saul in all his glory decided to take matters into his own hands. He ordered the remaining men to bring up burnt offerings and peace offerings in hopes that he might win the Lord's favor. It turns out that Saul spoke too soon, because immediately after he had finished with the offerings, Samuel showed up as promised.

You can imagine that Samuel, on his approach to the village, saw the massive billows of smoke arising from the burnt offerings in Gilgal. Saul went out to welcome Samuel, and we can further imagine that he believed Samuel's appearance was God's response to the burnt offerings he so wisely instructed his people to conduct.

Unfortunately for him, Samuel saw the bigger picture. "What on earth are you doing?!" Samuel asked.

And Saul replied, "When I saw I was losing my army from under me, *and* that you hadn't come when you said you would, *and* that the Philistines were poised at Micmash, I said, 'The Philistines are about to come down on me in Gilgal, and I haven't yet come before God asking for his help.' So I took things into my own hands and sacrificed the burnt offering."

Did you notice that? Saul immediately offers three excuses—three expectations that were not met; three reasons why he felt he ought to jump in and help God do His job.

"That was not smart, King Saul," Samuel said. "If you would have obeyed what the Lord God commanded of you, by now he would have established a firm and lasting foundation under your kingly rule over Israel. Your kingly rule is in shambles—if you couldn't tell by the thousands of men scattering from your side—all because you took matters into your own hands. For this, God has rejected you as king, and even now, is looking for your replacement!"

After that, Samuel got up and left Gilgal, leaving Saul to fend for himself. A mere six hundred men followed him from Gilgal towards Gibeah, where they would attempt to stage their defense against the monstrous Philistine army in what I like to call "The Battle of Miss-match." It must have been an incredibly awkward period, because Saul had just been told that his rule was quickly coming to an end, and the six hundred men were just waiting around for him to make a move.

Meanwhile, the Philistines were having a grand ol' time making sure the Israelites truly suffered humiliation under Saul's command. The Philistines were at such an advantage, not simply from a size standpoint, but also because of their superior weaponry. As such, the Philistines had made sure the Israelites didn't have a single blacksmith in their midst. Without blacksmiths to sharpen their weapons, Saul and Jonathan were the only men among the six hundred who were said to have swords and spears. And if that wasn't embarrassing enough, the Israelites even had to go to the Philistine blacksmiths just to sharpen their farming equipment, which, by the way, cost them an arm and a leg.

I would love to have been a fly on the tent wall of one of these Philistine blacksmiths while one of the Israelites was getting his sickle sharpened. The Philistine must have been smiling from ear to ear at the irony *he perceived* in the situation. "So, uh, your king . . . he's not too bright, is he?"

"Look, man, can we just keep this professional?"

"Oh, sure, sure. Yeah, it's just that, you know, you only have like six hundred men, and we've got, like, enough to number the sands of the seashore. I don't even know, to be honest with you, but we have a lot. Plus, we have weapons, you know, because we're going to fight, and weapons tend to aid in that sort of activity."

No matter how the conversations went, I'm sure it was awkward, and the Israelites were getting desperate. Fortunately for them, the apple fell far from the tree in that Jonathan was nothing like his father, Saul. Jonathan had the bright idea to go pick a fight with a garrison of Philistines who were camped on a distant ridge across a gorge. And while Jonathan's actions could be perceived as foolishly taking matters into his own hands the way his father had done, the difference here lies in where Jonathan placed his faith.

Jonathan turned to his armor bearer, who probably wasn't much older than a teenager, and said, "C'mon, let's go mess with these uncircumcised pagans on the other side of the pass. Perhaps God will move for us. After all, who says God can only deliver us with a big army? No one can stop God from saving whomever he pleases."

And his armor bearer replied, "Do all that is in your heart. Do as you wish, and you will see that I am with you heart and soul."

After that, they sneaked out of camp when no one was watching. Then they slipped through the cracks and crevices of the mountain until they were in the pass below and between the two armies. This is such a beautiful picture of faith and trust. While Jonathan's faith inspired courage in his armor bearer, we can still assume he was battling the doubts that were swirling in his head as they stepped into what would appear to be a suicide mission. After all, they only had a sword and a spear between the two of them. Still, the young man followed, bearing the weapon that belonged to his prince.

When they reached the bottom of the pass, Jonathan revealed his plan to his trusty servant as they hid behind a rock. "All right, listen, I know this sounds crazy, but we're going to cross over the pass and let the Philistines know we're down here. If they order us to stop until they come down to check us out, we'll stay put and not go up to them. But if they order us to come up, we'll know God has given them to us. That will be our sign, and up we go."

So they stepped out into the open, and the Philistines immediately started mocking them. "Check it out; the Hebrews are crawling out of their holes! Come on up here! We have something to show you!"

At this, Jonathan shouted, "Let's do this! God has delivered them into our hands!" and up they went, scrambling on all fours. When the Philistines came to oppose them, Jonathan plowed straight through them, knocking them on their backs. His armor bearer was right on his heels, finishing them off by bashing their heads in with stones.

In this first skirmish, Jonathan and his armor bearer killed about twenty men. The ground began to shudder, which set the surrounding encampments into a panic that eventually spread to the rest of the entire army.

Meanwhile, Saul discovered that his son had gone out from their camp and ordered his men to start attacking the Philistines. Upon doing so, they found that the Philistines were in such a panic that they had turned their swords on one another. The Israelites who had gone down to sharpen their tools began to slaughter the men in their confusion. Even the Hebrews who had run away to the surrounding towns started coming back to join the fight. The Philistines began to flee, and the battle passed on to the northwest. The mighty hand of the Lord, through the willingness of his humble servants, saved Israel that day.

Reading this story, as I did for so long, trying to figure out how applies to my life, I glazed over the true beauty of the story. At one point, I would have presumed we were all supposed to aspire to the character of Jonathan. After all, he was strong, bold, full of vigor, and trusted in the Lord. Any fourteen-year-old boy who's ever lived wishes they were able to plow through the upperclass bullies that mock him from the cliffs of lockers as he runs through the gauntlet on his way to P.E.

As I read the story now, I've still not been able to aspire to Jonathan's level of 'badass-etry.' I can certainly relate to King Saul's rashness, though I certainly don't want to end up as a lame duck king that cowardly falls on his own sword. I'm not old and grumpy enough yet to have much in common with Samuel, which really just leaves one more character through which we can observe this powerful story, and that is the armor bearer.

If this were a movie, the armor bearer would play the supporting cast member who follows the main character into battle. By himself, he does not have the faith or willingness to lead the charge. But he had most certainly been by Jonathan's side through many battles. He must have held his prince in the highest regard for not laughing in Jonathan's face when he suggested they go pick a fight with the overwhelming forces that surrounded them.

The armor bearer's response to the invitation is *almost* as outrageous as Jonathan's suggested course of action, but there's a big gap in that 'almost.' He says, "Come, let us cross over to the enemy. Perhaps the Lord will fight for us, for nothing can oppose the God of Israel when He desires to save His chosen people."

How does the armor bearer respond? He says, "Do all that is in your heart. Believe me, my heart and soul are in alignment with however you see fit to proceed."

And while Saul and the rest of the Israelite army ran,

hid, and waited to be starved out, Jonathan stepped toward danger, stepped into the chaos, and his armor bearer followed. Now if we are to play the armor bearer in this scenario, who, then, is to act as Jonathan?

From our own limited view, we would never be able to see that the star of this and every other story in the Bible is none other than Jesus himself. Everything points to the life, death, and resurrection of the Chosen One who willingly stepped into the chaos of this broken world in order that God might act on His behalf and save His chosen people. And just as happened in this particular battle, God moved mightily, resulting in panic in the minds of the enemy and leaving them to slaughter one another in their own confusion.

Not once did the armor bearer doubt or question his prince's intentions. With his imperfect perspective and a heart of trust, the armor bearer willingly followed one step at a time, and the battle was won.

But you might ask, "Well, if Jonathan truly had faith, then why did he say, '*Perhaps* God will move for us'?" And here lies the fascinating difference between Jonathan's faith and his father's lack thereof. You see, Saul was desperate. All he could perceive were the thousands of men leaving his side as the tremendous enemy army slowly surrounded him. He took it upon himself, thus, setting an expectation for how and when God would move. From this perspective, it all depended on him.

Jonathan, on the other hand, says, "Perhaps," meaning "If the Lord wants to move through us, He will do so, for nothing can stop His hand from accomplishing what He wills." He makes himself available without setting expectations. Now Jonathan and his armor bearer become vessels, which the Spirit of God chose to pour into. God blessed his open heart and willingness to take a step. Saul essentially attempted to force God's hand and was rejected as king because of it. In his place, God chose another man (boy) after His own heart, and it's no wonder Jonathan and King David were soon to become as close as brothers.

THE BIGGER PICTURE INCLUDES WHAT God has in plan for us, and we don't need to see the bigger picture in order to live within it. If we believe in our heart of hearts that God's plan for us is not for our demise but for our prosperity, our current and false reality of a life without him is miraculously reverted back to its true and original design. Our hearts are turned to God, and we begin more and more to look for Him to provide all that we need instead of our grasping and groping for something that we already truly have.

This doesn't mean that we just walk through our lives in voluntary ignorance. God invites us to "work out our salvation," not to be confused with "saving ourselves." But if we use the minds we've been given to explore the mystery of the love He speaks to our hearts, we discover an enchanted world where all of creation shimmers and glistens with the hopeful longing to return to the Garden. We don't need to live in a perfect world in order to enjoy the peace we hope for in a perfect world. The peace that flows out of the Spirit dwelling in our heart is available to us at any and every moment. If Christ lives within us, His power covers us, and we can essentially respond to His invitation to re-enter into the Garden at will. Sadly, because we don't live in a perfect world, our minds are often drawn out of the Garden and we begin to doubt that we have everything we need.

This is why training is essential. If we allow God to lead us according to the bigger picture that only He can see, we begin to trust Him more and more. We awaken to His voice, realizing He has always been with us, even in the moments when our minds run away in search of some better joy. But as we learn to willfully submit to His voice, we find we don't have to worry about the perils that will inevitably arise in the adventure ahead. He is fully aware of them and can guide us through them if we're willing to stay in stride with Him in the present moment.

Yonah warming in the sun after a cold swim.

Yonah splashing through the shoals at Seven Islands.

5

The Perils of Adventure

"Adventure is not outside a man; it is within."
—Mary Anne Evans, English novelist
(Under the pen name George Eliot)

N OW THAT YONAH IS A BIT OLDER, he's becoming the perfect adventure companion. I know his tendencies, and I know I can trust him to listen to my voice. Like any great adventure buddy, he's up for whatever type of adventure I have in mind. No matter where we go, he is determined to explore all it has to offer, and I've found myself in some special places because of his unquenchable thirst for adventure. But of all the places we've ever adventured, the bird sanctuary across the river from our cabin was by far his favorite. I know this because he told me.

Seven Islands Bird Sanctuary is a mystical place. If for no other reason, go there to confirm that there are, in fact, seven islands. The three largest islands basically split the river in half and run about the length of a mile. From where we put in on the southern shore, we only have to paddle upriver about a hundred yards to round the point of the first island and turn downstream to begin circling the islands.

Typically, we'll paddle up to the point, and the quickness of the river's current that day will determine how many islands we'll pass before we loop around and head back up river. As long as it hasn't rained too much, the river stays pretty shallow, and there's only a few points where I'll have to get out and walk the boat up the rapids. If the river is running too high, I'll actually have to pull the boat out at some point downriver on the south shore and walk back up to my car.

On this particular day, I decided to drag the boat upriver with Yonah in tow. The water wasn't too high, and I was eager to see the river otters that tend to come out and play on days like this. On the way up, Yonah spotted a flock of geese about a hundred yards up and jumped out of the boat. At first, I was tempted to stop him, knowing the river was a bit higher than I was comfortable with. But my selfishness got the best of me. I decided his struggle against the current would wear him down, making him much more enjoyable to be around later that night. (I know all dogs are pretty dang cute when they're tired, but Yonah definitely takes the cake. If you think your pup is cuter, write your own book about it.)

Anyway, Yonah took off after the geese, who honked in terror and took flight at the first sight of this monstrous puppy splashing up the river toward them. They weren't too alarmed, though, and settled back into the shallows another twenty yards upriver. This game of dog-and-goose only intensified Yonah's urge to greet them. This cycle repeated a couple times, and I knew the river well enough to see that they were about to leave the shallows. I yelled for Yonah to stop and come back, but his eager splashing drowned out my call as he headed straight for the deeper waters.

I smiled and shook my head, knowing exactly what Yonah was about to get himself into. In anticipation, I waded out into the deeper water a hundred yards or so downriver. He, of course, pursued them as deep as he could, but as his paws left the ground, he was immediately swept up in the current.

And what do ya know? Here comes Yonah floating

straight toward me. As he came closer, I could see the panic in his eyes, as if to say, "Help me, Dad; I had no idea the river was going to sweep me off my paws!"

I calmly grabbed him by the scruff of his neck and effortlessly pulled him to the safety of the boat.

I got you, homie, I thought as I made my way back to the shallows. He sat there shivering and out of breath. Captivated by the thrill of the hunt, he had forgotten all about me, and it wasn't until he needed help did he remember to look for me.

For most of my life, my relationship with God was much like the way Yonah jumped out of the boat to chase the geese. From the moment he saw them, he forgot all about me until he got himself in a bind and very much needed me to pull him out. In the same way, I only cried out to God when I was in trouble. Being the loving Father that He is, God is always eager to rescue His children. But because He is such a loving Father, He desires a much fuller, richer relationship with us that is simply not possible if He only comes to the front of our mind when we urgently need something.

Because of my stubborn nature, I was stuck in this elementary level of our relationship for most of my life. I was aware of my desire for Him, but I insisted that our relationship be on my terms, which I now know is laughably ridiculous to even consider. God doesn't exist on anyone's terms, and to do so would confine Him to some idea or picture of whatever we believe He should look like.

This is a tough pill for many of us to swallow. We want to be able to fit God into a box and store it away until we need something, then we can take the box off the shelf and open it up at will. This is a despairingly sad perspective of a relationship with God. In fact, it's not really a relationship at all. Keep in mind that the only thing God ever wants from us, the very reason He created us, was so that we could live in relationship with Him, or them (the Trinity). When we stuff God in a box, we forget that we were made for God, not the other way around.

But God never forgets this. He loves me enough to give me what I truly need instead of what I believe I need. He also knew that I would become so frustrated with my petty attempts to live life on my terms that I'd eventually throw up my hands in surrender, which happened precisely the moment I stepped off the balcony.

Now that my newly surrendered heart was in a position to listen, the Gardener began to cultivate the landscape of my heart. Jesus began to speak to me about many of the wounds I'd been carrying around for decades and that avoiding these wounds not only prolonged the pain but actually intensified their power over my thoughts and actions. I was trying to act like they weren't there. However they were consuming my entire nature all the while with lie after lie about who I was and who I needed to be.

But as Jesus began to till the soil in my garden, He broke up many of the hardened lies I'd been believing about what a garden is supposed to look like. He showed me that no two gardens are alike. He has a very special plan to bring forth beauty and life from a garden that once resembled a desert. Wound by wound, lie by lie, He touched those places in my heart and spoke His love over them. Just as He did with His doubt-filled disciple, Thomas, Jesus invited me to touch the scars in His hands and feet—the scars that He signed up for so that He could enter my garden and lay out an entirely new vision for what it would look like.

As he continued his good work in my heart, those wounds began to heal, the pain lost its sting, and I no longer felt compelled to hide or avoid them. Miraculously, as they turned to scars, I became grateful for them. Each and every one of them is a reminder of who I truly am. More importantly, they are proof in my life that Jesus is who He says He is. He not only invited me to touch the scars in His hands and feet, but would later give me the honor of being those hands and feet, carrying His message of love to all those who feel lost and powerless.

At the time, as I stood there in the garden with Him while He worked, I was able to talk to Him about many of the fears and doubts that infested my garden in the first place. Interestingly enough, many of them were still there, but now that I was comfortable allowing Jesus to walk through it with me, they didn't seem quite so scary. I no longer felt like I needed to avoid or cover them.

"*Jesus, what about this plant here? It's all shriveled up and looks kind of dead. Shouldn't we just rip it out of the ground and toss it in the burn pile?*"

Jesus would smile and kneel down next to it with his pruning shears.

"*I suppose we could do that if you really want to, but would you believe that it's actually a rare flower?*

"*Really, that ugly thing is a* rare *flower?*"

"*Yep, and it blossoms in the most beautiful and vibrant colors. I know it looks dead right now, but with a little bit of nurturing, some day you might find that it is one of the most beautiful plants in this whole garden.*"

"*If you say so . . .* " I say and shrug my shoulders as He begins to prune the plant's leaves back.

"*You see, this plant's leaves grew too large and were absorbing so much of the nutrients that it wasn't able to blossom. So, if I prune off some of the leaves, the nutrients from the root can now be directed toward the fruit. Trust me, next time you see it, you'll hardly be able to recognize it.*"

The Thrill of the Hunt

This picture of the way Jesus longs to walk with us through the garden of our hearts is beautifully reminiscent of life before the Fall. Now that the garden has come under the curse of sin, I find it fascinating that Jesus still wants to stroll through the garden and even more so that He doesn't want to do it without us. From our lowly, worldly view, it would be entirely plausible to view Jesus as a Haz-Mat worker that comes in, ropes off our hearts as a disaster zone, and goes to work on cleaning up the garden, preferring us to stay as far away as possible so as not to further mess things up.

But this is so far removed from who Jesus actually is. As I'm getting to know Him more and more, I'm learning how eager He is to give us a tour of our own garden, even in its messy state. Furthermore, like so many others, I had learned to see my garden as something I needed to tidy up and make presentable before I invited Jesus to walk in it. I believed then, and only then, would I be worthy of receiving His approval and favor. I exhausted myself, trying to make my garden appear pristine on the surface while I ignored the root issues. Whenever I looked up to examine my handiwork, I'd often find that the weeds had already grown back and the thorns hindered me from reaching many of the areas that I thought needed the most work. I quickly lost heart and wondered, *What's the use in gardening if the flowers never blossom or the trees never bear fruit?*

But the moment Jesus stepped foot in my garden, He began to show me how He views it. Because I had believed for so long that I needed to make it presentable for Jesus to approve of it, I was extremely surprised to learn that He didn't want to set it ablaze and completely start anew. Instead, His exceedingly peaceful, loving nature created a safe space for me to simply ask questions about what I saw and had been experiencing within my garden. I was finally able to be honest with him, questioning the shame I felt and had even tried to hide from Him.

He also showed me the danger of labeling my garden according to what the eyes of my fleshly mind can see. We humans have a terrible tendency to assign labels to things we deem as 'good' or 'bad' and to proceed according to our lowly perspective. But this, too, is a form of control and it restricts the object we're labeling to what we can see about it rather than what it truly is. Labels serve the ego because we naturally want to align ourselves with the things we deem as 'good' and avoid those we see as 'bad.' In doing so, we attempt to justify our actions and earn our salvation. I don't know about you, but this hasn't worked out so well for me in the past.

By their nature, labels confine the object of our eye to whatever the brain is able to perceive and comprehend about it at a given moment (which we know to be extremely limited).

When we do this, we sadly miss out on everything else this object has to offer.

Consider a work of art. Because of its transcendent qualities, art is often valued because it is open to the observer's interpretation. We, of course, gravitate to a piece that speaks to us and might shun one that we don't have a connection to. The issue with this outlook is that it completely neglects the artist, who designed and labored over the piece in making it exactly what it is. The work came out of a place in their own mind and heart, and whether is speaks to yours should not have any effect on its value.

Similarly, a friend of mine once told me about the time her parents took her to visit Japan when she was a young girl. Like many of us when we were young, she refused to try any of the 'strange' foods available in this foreign country. No matter what her parents offered her, she absolutely would not swallow it, and she ate nothing but rice during her three-week stay. When she finally returned home, she was extremely malnourished. She was young and, of course, didn't know any better, but I wonder if we're not so different when we assign labels to things and refuse to partake in anything that does not suit our palette. We are satisfied with only a fraction of the life available to us. Out of both arrogance and ignorance, our sight is limited to such a narrow view.

This is the danger of labels. Our brains are a gift, and they are designed to help us efficiently complete the various tasks our lives require of us throughout the day. But that's it; that's where the brain's job description ends. To enlist the brain's assistance in areas where it doesn't have clearance is to neglect the clear boundaries that it is designed to enhance.

ONE PARTICULARLY BUSY WORK WEEK during the summer, I brought Yonah into town with the intention of taking him to a park along the Tennessee River. It had been a beautiful morning, and I was excited to get out of the office and take a stroll along the shoreline. Even more so, I was doubly excited for Yonah to get some much-needed exercise.

Literally the moment I left the office and got into my car, a summer storm blew in out of nowhere and released a torrential downpour across the foreseeable future. I, of course, became immediately frustrated, largely because I had built up the perfect afternoon in my mind. I expected it to be a gorgeous afternoon when I left work. As the storm rolled in, my mind's eye saw it as ruined.

Perhaps out of the same stubbornness that has plagued me most of my life, I determined to go to the park, anyway. Upon arrival, Yonah leaped from the car, just as I would have expected him to do if it had not been raining. Even still, I expected him to run around for a few minutes until deciding he wasn't in the mood to get wet and eventually mope back to the car with the shivers. But no, he ignored the rain and darted around the open park like a cow in a tornado and reminded me just how much of a puppy he still was.

What in the world has gotten into him? I wondered from across the field.

As he came closer, I began to realize he was flushing birds out of every nook 'n cranny in the field.

OK, what has gotten into these birds? Surely in this rain, they . . . Then I realized, When it rains, the worms are flushed out of the ground, enticing the birds out of the tree, which means . . . it's a bird dog's wet dream! I reveled as the rain began to dwindle.

With this realization, I immediately joined in Yonah's bliss. Bless his heart! He probably thought this was all part of my elaborate plan to surprise him with the best afternoon his short-term memory could muster. I smiled, knowing I should strive to be more like Yonah.

Because I was so quick to label the rainy afternoon as ruined, I nearly missed this wonderful experience I got to share with my dog, just as I nearly missed a special moment of insight from my God.

LOOKING BACK, IT'S EASY TO see why I labeled my garden as 'shameful' or 'unlovable' because I labeled Jesus as a God who wanted to shame me into obedience. In doing so, I hid from Him in the shadows and anxiously waited for Him to pass by as He walked through my garden calling my name.

But I eventually grew so desperate for my life to look different that I no longer cared what Jesus or anyone else had to say about it. I just didn't want to hide anymore, and I slowly grew more comfortable with allowing Jesus into many of the disgusting corners of my heart. I was shocked to learn that it was me who despised my garden, not Him. It was me who wanted to burn the garden and start over, while He had incredible plans to use even the messiest parts of it for His glory.

As He continues to nurture and heal my heart, I can now celebrate what Jesus is doing in my life, and I share it with others. After all, the opposite of hiding something is to celebrate it. When I talk about these tiny miracles with my brothers and sisters around me, I get to hear what Jesus is doing in their hearts, and I am continually perplexed by the commonalities of our fears and struggles. They might manifest themselves in different ways, but at their root, they are so incredibly similar. We all want and need love. We all want acceptance, affirmation, and the safety that comes from belonging to a community. We all encounter the tension that naturally arises from a world that tells us that if we work hard enough on our image, then we will earn that love and be free. But as we share these struggles, I realize we're all just scratching our heads, wondering how we've worked so hard to perfect our ourselves only to still feel the sting of rejection.

Together, we can learn to let go of that misconception; it's a heavy burden that is not intended for us. God doesn't expect us to maintain a perfect garden; otherwise, He would not have entered into the brokenness of the world for the purpose of saving it. In fact, God doesn't expect us to do anything; He only invites us to enter into what is best for us. We are fully loved and fully accepted, and nothing can add to or take away from that reality. The relief that comes from knowing we don't have to bear this impossible weight will forever bring tears of wonder-filled joy to my eyes. The degree to which we want to live out the fullness of life, well, now that is entirely up to us, and there is a magnificent paradox that comes along that is built into the perils of our great adventure—we choose both our freedoms and our chains.

Knowing that we're all children of God and that nothing else could define us, we are free to come and go as we are—with all of our doubts, fears, wounds, and failures. This freedom enables us to address the tension in our hearts without the need to fix or control it, though it is deeply woven into our flesh that we attempt to do so. But the mere awareness of this freedom is enough to open our hearts to receive what Jesus has to say about it, and that, my friends, is worth eternal celebration.

Kahlil Gibran, the twentieth-century mystic and poet from Lebanon (and one of my favorite writers) proses about this same freedom:

> "Ay, in the grove of the temple and in the shadow of the citadel, I have seen the freest among you wear their freedom as a yoke and a handcuff. And my heart bled within me; for you can only be free when even the desire for freedom becomes a harness to you, and when you cease to speak of freedom as a goal and a fulfillment.

> "You shall be free indeed when your days are not without a care nor your nights without a want and a grief, but rather, when these things girdle your life and yet you rise above them naked and unbound.

> "And how shall you rise beyond your days and nights unless you break the chains which you at the dawn of your understanding have fastened around your noon hour? In truth that which you call freedom is the strongest of these chains, though its links glitter in the sun and dazzle your eyes.

"And what is it but fragments of your own self you would discard that you may become free?

" . . . And if it is a care that you would cast off, that care has been chosen by you rather than imposed upon you. And if it is a fear that you would dispel, the seat of that fear is in your heart and not in the hand of the feared.

"Verily, all these things move within your being in constant half embrace, the desired and the dreaded, the repugnant and the cherished, the pursued and that which you would escape.

"These things move within you as lights and shadows in pairs that cling. And when the shadow fades and is no more, the light that lingers becomes a shadow to another light.

"And thus your freedom when it loses its fetters becomes itself a fetter of a greater freedom."[1]

Yonah's game of dog-and-goose on the river that day might have continued without end if Yonah hadn't been swept away by the river's current. No matter how eager he was to get close to the flock of geese, they'd have to be half-asleep or honking up a storm to not notice the four-legged frenzy splashing up the river toward them. Yonah might as well have been chasing his tail, or, as the qoheleth put it in Ecclesiastes, striving after the wind.

Fortunately, I had the foresight to see what was about to take place. And I was able to position myself where I could rescue my overly excited puppy from being washed farther downriver. If I had not been paying attention or if I had been unable to get in position in time, Yonah could have easily been swept past me, and we would have had a whole other situation on our hands.

God used this event to illustrate the perils that inevitably arise from living this adventure from my mind rather than from my heart. Trying to address the weeds and thorns in my overgrown garden by myself left me exhausted and despairingly alone. I, like Yonah, am unable to see life from the bigger picture. Not only is my vision too limited, but it's not really my job in the first place. That's God's job, and He takes great pleasure in doing it exceedingly well.

Thankfully, because His vision is so infinitely more perceptible than mine, He pointed out how dangerous it is to see my life as something I can control. While it was extremely painful to learn that I am simply unable to control the events of my life, it was incredibly relieving to learn that God doesn't expect His children to do so. This false sense of control is nothing more than an exercise in futility, and it breaks God's heart to watch myself and so many of His children suffer under the bondage of that illusion.

Fortunately, He has a couple tricks up his sleeve to dismantle this illusion. Unfortunately, those tricks can be rather painful, and just like Yonah's getting a choice in the intensity of his training, we also get a choice in the degree of pain we undergo.

"Any individual—human or canine—who grows up getting whatever he wants virtually every time he wants it is going to mature into an individual who has no tolerance for frustration. After all, frustration derives from expectations." [2]

—Patricia B. McConnell, PhD.,
author of *The Other End of the Leash*

I've long had a fascination with expectations. They almost

Yonah manning his post from the top floor of our cabin. No suspicious activity reported that day.

always go unspoken and are most often based on the assumption that one can read another's mind. Even more perplexing is the fact that expectations, because of their assumptive nature, are often only discovered after they have failed to be met.

To give you an example, recall Chipper, the second GSP I had in my early twenties. At that time, I was fortunate to have a job where I could bring Chipper to work. One day, I needed to drop off a package at the post office a few blocks from our downtown office. I figured it was the perfect opportunity to kill two birds with one stone, in that I could take Chipper for a walk while conveniently running an overdue errand.

We strolled the half mile or so across town, where I tied Chipper's leash to a parking meter just outside the entrance to the post office. I stepped inside and began to peruse the envelope stand in search of the perfect envelope for my fancy, oldtimey snail mail. After choosing one and filling out the mailing address, I stepped into the snail line and patiently waited to be called to the counter.

Next thing I know, I heard gasps of laughter coming from the folks in line behind me. I turned around to find Chipper darting about the post office lobby with about ten inches of his chewed-up leash in tow. My heart skipped a beat and the blood rushed to my head as I blushed my way through the lobby trying to contain this Tasmanian devil.

Fortunately, no individual—human or canine—had ever attempted to sneak *into* the post office and the folks behind the counter were quite gracious while allowing me to mail my letter with a puppy under my arm. I thanked them for their kindness and headed outside to retrieve the other end of the leash.

As I recall that silly moment in the post office, Chipper and I had two very different expectations for what was supposed to happen. Tying him up to the parking meter, I expected him to stay there until I came back. From my perspective, I trusted the leash to hold him in place and was willing to wager that the parking meter wasn't going to take him for a walk around the block while I was inside. However, Chipper (whose name is, again, perfect for this illustration) expected that the same master taking him on a walk would have the decency to bring him inside to see what a post office looks like. Either way, I realized we failed to meet each other's expectations the moment he came barreling into the post office lobby.

From the shattering of our expectations arose a tension in each individual. Chipper grew so distressed as to gnaw through an inch-wide polyester/cotton-blended leash like a hot knife through butter. My failed expectation caused me to blush with embarrassment because I was afraid people might suspect me of being an irresponsible dog owner (which I undoubtedly was at the time). The petty fear irked me and was the sort of recurring instance that enslaved me to a life of apprehension and subsequent attempts to escape that feeling.

Why was I putting that pressure on myself? No one in the post office cared. In fact, it probably brightened their day. But for someone who was as self-absorbed as I was then, all I could think about was how embarrassingly frustrated I was. My anxiety spiked (along with my blood pressure) alerting me that something was wrong. Since I was only looking at myself, I had every reason to suspect that something was wrong with me. I felt like I had a disease and that this incident would finally be the moment that my sickness was unveiled to the world. My greatest fear, of course, was failing to meet the world's expectations of being a fully put-together twenty-four-year-old, or perhaps that was my expectation that I projected onto the world. That sort of pressure is enough to spike the anxiety level of a person of any age.

I listened to a podcast a few years ago that forever changed my perspective of anxiety. I later became extremely grateful for its timing in my life, as I heard it right at the onset of my most emotionally trying years.

In this podcast, the psychologist being interviewed made the fascinating claim that anxiety is essential to life. He set up his illustration by discussing the various emotions a mother will experience after she discovers she is with child. Of course, she might be excited at the thought of being a mother, but as her due date draws near, she might begin to experience fear and doubt. Perhaps she fears she might be inadequate to properly care for this bright-eyed ball of flesh and need. Later, she might feel conflicted about her decision to bring a child into an increasingly cruel world. All the while, these various emotions intertwine with her inexplicable curiosity at the thought of bringing forth life.

The psychologist goes on to explain how sensitive the unborn child is to the various emotions of its mother. Inside the womb, the child is learning her mother's voice and is continually dependent on her for everything—for nutrition, protection, even down to the very breath her mother takes in.

As is the *natural order*, the time eventually comes for the baby to leave the womb and enter this great big world. At this time, both the mother and the child must make a decision, even if only in their subconscious, and it is within the birth canal that the anxiety that's been building for the past nine months now comes to a head.

If the mother, perhaps out of anxious fear of the immense pain, neglects the natural process, the child will die inside of her. If the child, perhaps out of anxious fear of her present world passing away, chooses to resist and stay inside the womb, both she and her mother could die during birth.

The Thrill of the Hunt

But, if the child and her mother submit to the *natural process* regardless of the anxiety and immense pain they will inevitably undergo, life is brought forth, much to the relief and joy of them both. And from the very first moment the mother looks into the eyes of her beautiful baby girl, all the fears and anxious thoughts evaporate because she now holds the mystery of life in her tired arms.

I love this illustration for two reasons. One, because I doubt I'll ever experience the degree of anxiety and pain that a mother must go through in order to bring life into the world. Second, although I don't remember it, I'm told I have experienced all this from the baby's perspective, and the event is now left up to my imagination to dramatize the tension.

Within this beaker-shaped birth canal in my mind, I imagine flashing red lights, sirens and screams piercing through the darkness. I am acutely aware that something is changing, and I feel my heartbeat racing as I realize for the first time that my mother's and my heartbeats are not actually one and the same. I descend further down the canal; my body shivers at the cold air that grips my flesh for the first time, and suddenly, a burst of white light envelops my world. The sound is deafening, and I shriek in terror. Thankfully, a pair of warm hands gently wraps a soft fabric around my cold skin and, for a moment, it reminds me of the comfort of my mother's womb. I grow warmer still as I'm placed between my mother's breasts, and the sound of *her* heartbeat once again soothes me into my new life. It's all over, or maybe it's just begun.

IN MY RESEARCH FOR THIS BOOK, I came across a fascinating similarity that we humans share with our canine companions. When humans gaze into one another's eyes, say, a moment shared between lovers, or a mother staring into the eyes of her child, the bond between them is reinforced due to a hormone released in the brain known as *oxytocin*. (If you can't tell, I find the intricacies of the human body to be enchanting.)

But would you believe that the same bond is formed when a dog gazes into the eyes of its master? Scientists say that mutual gazing increases oxytocin levels in humans, and when the dog catches the scent of its master's oxytocin, the dog in turn gazes back, as if magnetically. The effect is referred to as the "oxytocin-gaze positive loop," and is believed to have strongly contributed to the coevolution of human-canine bonds for millennia. Wolves, on the other, rarely make eye contact with their handlers and are, thus, seemingly resistant to this effect.

More fascinating, still, is that the same process happens when humans engage with their Master, a practice known as prayer. It would appear that we are made for and strengthened by that bond.

My friends, I pray we can all begin to see the perils of journeying alone and neglecting the guidance of our Master. I pray when we hear that we are "fearfully and wonderfully made," we can trust that our minds are a beautiful gift and allow us to enjoy the endless blessings that hang from the many trees in our garden. But as we consider which of those fruits to enjoy, we must understand the limits of our perception. Our minds are *not*, as the serpent would have us believe, meant to keep us from being "like God." We already are "like God" because we are entirely made in the image of and for God, and we would all do well to remember the freedom that is contained within this mysterious relationship.

So what are our minds meant for?

Well, we know the brain is terrifically complex, but it actually exists for the simple purpose of perceiving a situation. As we digest the information, we register what most immediately affects our well-being, discard that which does not, and formulate a reaction that best increases our chances for survival. Where it becomes highly complex is when we add in memory (experience) and subconsciously project possible dangers into our past or future. We try to justify ourselves in events that have already happened and defend ourselves from potential dangers from events that haven't even taken place yet.

As essential as it was to the survival of Knubby and his caveman homies in meeting their primal needs, the mind can cause serious problems in the highly complex world of today. We often get ourselves in trouble at the onset of a situation because we believe the way we have viewed a certain problem is the *only* way it can be perceived. In other words, we trust the analysis of our brain to sufficiently preserve our individual wellness.

In this natural process of the mind, the brain's analysis leads us to label a subject 'good' or 'bad.' The labels we assign create expectations for ourselves and our circumstances. Expectations are an illusion of perfection that we project into the future, saying "If I don't experience _____when _____ happens, then I will be _____." By posing this scenario, we are essentially saying that if we cannot control our situations ('bad') and force our desired outcome ('good'), then we are surely [insert your worst fear here].

We humans don't do a very good job of looking into the future, and, therefore, expectations must either be exceeded or fallen short of, and the universe that hangs in that balance is called tension. It's a grave peril of the adventure, and it's the very reason our western society is plagued by anxiety.

We enter into a situation we have yet to master and, because we don't understand it, we fear it. As such, we allow it to overpower us, and we wallow in the tension. We were perfectly designed for perfection, and our hearts recognize glimpses of home. But as we go about our days, we insist that our lives should reflect that vision, all the while forgetting the simple reality that we forfeited our true nature and left our home long, long ago.

But herein lies the good news. God does not want us to forfeit our true nature, and He devised a plan in which He would enter into this crazy tension and prove that we are more lovable than anything we could ever imagine. Heaven came down to earth for the sole purpose of convincing all of Creation that we are His treasured children, and He will allow nothing to stand in His way.

Through the life of Jesus, our God insists that we know this Truth, and as any good Father, He is willing to train us to see the perils of our adventure. In doing so, He creates boundaries that are not only good for preserving the natural order of His design, but also for enabling us to prosper beyond our wildest imagination.

YONAH HATES CHORES, NOT BECAUSE I make him do them, but because they postpone his playtime. He follows me around the house, positioning himself in my way so as to remove all doubt of his intentions to thwart my responsibilities. I'll be sweeping in the kitchen and turn to find him scowling at me from the foyer. When I do the dishes, he wonders why on earth I'd need anything more than one bowl for food and one bowl for water. To him, any move I make is a potential step toward the door, and a step toward the door, of course, means playtime.

One beautiful autumn morning, he was especially frustrated with my rare decision to do chores. He whined and whimpered from the foyer, but the sun was shining, the music was blaring, and it was just one of those mornings when the looming of overdue chores was victorious over my devout procrastination.

As I turned from one chore to the next, I nearly tripped over him more than a few times. Finally, I danced over and cradled him from behind, forcing him to dance with me.

"Be patient, Bubba," I said. "We'll go play in just a little bit. If you helped me clean instead of shedding your fur and making a mess everywhere you go in this house, chore time would be over much quicker."

Yonah leaves a mess practically everywhere he goes. Whether it's his constant shedding or the trail of water he leaves within a twenty-foot radius of his bowl, one thing is for sure—he does *not* help me clean. And as I was reminding Yonah of this, God tapped me on the shoulder and reminded *me* that maybe I'm not so different.

The thought might have gone over my head if I'd not had a strange prodding only minutes earlier while scrubbing the toilet. That's when I realized how ironic it is that the room we use to clean ourselves is the same room we use to discard our waste, and it happens to be the grossest room in the house. We humans can be disgusting. Our hairs fall out, filling every nook and cranny in the bathroom, and our decaying skin cells are constantly collecting on every level surface. We call it "gunk," but it's humanity at its finest . . . and there's a strange beauty in that. It's the daily manifestation of the tension that arises between our mortal bodies and our eternal selves.

Imagine what would happen if we tried to cover up or control this disgusting reality. We would literally spend every second of our lives moisturizing our skin and dusting every level surface we crossed. That sounds exhausting. I don't know about you, but I've resolved to accept my inability to stop myself from shedding skin cells and leaving gunk on everything we touch. Furthermore, I'm perplexed by this mystery. Seems to me like we'd have run out of skin cells by now. Yet there's this little phenomenon we all take for granted called regeneration. By no effort of our own, our skin cells are replenished, keeping our insides from oozing out onto the carpet. This all happens without our constant recognition and makes the continuation of life possible.

In fact, the mystery of regeneration is *life,* I thought as I finished my chores and headed outside with Yonah for another adventure. I smiled, knowing I'd just had a touch from Jesus that penetrated the boundaries of my awareness. Heaven met the earth in the most miniscule of chores, and that was enough to set my day on fire.

Yonah soaking up some sand and a sunset.

6

The Freedom of Boundaries

"If you're not free not to, then you're not free."

— Anonymous

L IKE DISCIPLINE, BOUNDARIES GET A BAD RAP THESE DAYS and are largely misunderstood. The current of counterculture is on the rise, now more than ever, and is constantly blurring the boundary line between what is acceptable and unacceptable. As history proves, a new boundary is drawn out of the confusion of the blur, and we call that process "progress."

Oh, but we like the word *progress*, don't we? It strokes our societal ego and gives us the illusion that we're in control and moving forward. Well, true progress comes from reshaping, which is synonymous with training, and we've already established that discipline *is* training. So maybe boundaries aren't so bad after all?

A boundary is a point of reference, and boundaries exist in all areas of our lives. We have traffic lanes to keep cars moving as safely and efficiently as possible. Many countries don't have them; even riding in a taxi in such places can be terribly frightening for someone who's not used to it. We also have imaginary boundaries called laws that are generally agreed upon by the members of a community to uphold the shared values. Of course, not everyone has the same values, which is why wars often break out.

Not only are boundaries vital for the well-being of the greater good, they are the single most important aspect of any form of training and are the driving force behind any hope of progression. An athlete is constantly aware of the boundaries of his or her ability, yet the point of training is to break through the old boundary and establish a new boundary. A trainee often finds oneself frustrated with a trainer's persistent encouragement even after one feels a limit has been reached.

But again, this is the point of having a trainer who sees your potential, sees an inner strength that one might not see in oneself, and finds a way to convince the trainee that the goal is still worth pursuing. *"Trust the process,"* the trainer might say. *"This is the only way."*

GROWING UP, CHIP WAS MOSTLY an outside dog. When we were home, the only room he was allowed in was the kitchen. It blew my young mind how my Dad was able to convince him not to enter into the adjacent dining or living rooms. At that age, I had no idea the extent of a dog's territorial awareness or its desire to please its master.

Chip's bed was in the garage, and I remember going out to hug him every night just before bedtime. At the time, I thought he might be lonely having to sleep in the garage all by himself. In hindsight, he was probably thrilled at the chance for some peace and quiet. When we were gone during the day, we'd crack the garage door and allow him to come and go as he wanted, so long as he minded the electric fence and stayed on our property.

It didn't happen often, but I recall several times on our way home from school when we'd pull into the neighborhood and catch a glimpse of Chip darting in between our neighbors' houses. He had escaped during the day and was out on some glorious adventure. A couple times, he'd even cross the street right in front of our car, and we'd stop and yell for him. When he realized it was his family, and more importantly, that he was not where he was supposed to be, he'd dart back home through the network of back yards and, upon our arrival, act like he'd been there the whole time.

I always got a kick out of the thought of him contemplating his escape during our absence. I'd helped Dad train him with the electric fence, and I knew Chip enjoyed the shock sensation about as much as you or I enjoy stubbing our toes on the dining room table. He'd whimper and whine whenever we'd be playing in the neighbor's yard and he was stuck in ours, but no matter how much fun we were having, he wouldn't dare leave the property if we were in sight.

(Side note: I think stubbing our toes is quite comedic. We can't even walk through a room without being distracted. What does that tell you about our minds?)

Knowing how much Chip disliked the shock, it always perplexed me to find him out perusing the neighborhood. What was it outside our yard that enticed him so much that he would endure the painful shock? And perhaps more interestingly, why did he only leave the yard at the times when he knew no one was home?

As I mentioned in previous chapters, rules and boundaries have never been my strong suit; until recently, I've always had a pretty unhealthy relationship with them. I saw rules as an obstacle standing in the way of my getting what I wanted. They were uncomfortable, controlling, and existed for the explicit purpose of limiting my entitled freedom. But not so long ago I was given eyes to see that I'd had a gross misunderstanding of their nature.

As I became more aware of life outside my family, it didn't take long for me to realize that my household rules were quite different from those I saw in the families around me. Once I learned that those rules could be craftily broken, I got really clever at toeing the line. I never quite reached the level of taking pleasure out of deliberate disobedience; it was more like I adhered to the rules I agreed with and didn't bat an eyelash at breaking the ones that kept me from getting what I wanted.

Our family had all sorts of weird rules, many of which I'm now thankful for but were painfully confusing at the time. I can still shock a room when I attempt to explain why we weren't bestowed the normal childhood luxuries such as *Scooby-Doo* and *Rugrats*. Furthermore, we were only allowed to play videogames on the weekends, and there was a period when even those were limited to a single hour a day. During the summers, my brothers and I were forbidden to be at the pool from 11 A.M. to 3 P.M. because that was when the sun was most dangerous to our pale Anglo-Saxon skin. This reality was devastating to any ten-year-old who understands that this particular four-hour block of time is precisely the time of day for which a pool was invented. Many of the rules we begrudgingly obeyed were laughable. As such, they were laughed at . . . a lot.

When you're five or six, rules are just rules and everybody's are the same. But as I got a bit older, I began to see that we were the weird, sheltered family; that simply would not do. I was tired of being laughed at, tired of feeling excluded. I started to resent the rules; then I resented the other kids for not having my set of rules; then I resented my parents for making my set of rules; then, only then, would I begin to resent myself for not breaking them.

I grew skeptical of rules and, instead of questioning their existence, I often ignored them. I think my family's rules were one of the first insecurities I can recall having.

(Except, of course, the first and only time I made the mistake of wearing tear-away gym pants during a flag football game against First Apostolic Church. Let's just say I wish I'd known about boxer briefs in sixth grade because, apparently, whitey-tighties were no longer considered socially acceptable.)

Yep, there's no avoiding it—rules suck when you're a kid—and I quickly began to suck at keeping them. My misunderstanding of rules would wreak havoc on the next fifteen to twenty years of my life. I hurt myself and countless people by not giving them the respect they deserved. During those years, I had to learn a couple important lessons about rules, and I had to learn them the hard way.

First, a rule must be attended to if for no other purpose than to establish a point of reference for one's desire, one's priority. At the risk of diving into behavioral psychology of a dog (a field about which I know very little), let's use the example of the invisible fence in my childhood yard. As Chip was stuck on our property and looking through the invisible fence at the wide world of adventure on the other side, we can imagine him calculating the shock-to-adventure ratio before venturing across the line. The invisible fence has now become a point of reference for Chip to gauge his priorities. He can either obey and be stuck in the yard, or absorb the shock and dig his claws into some real adventure. I've seen this same drama play out time and time again in my life, but we'll talk more about that in a moment. For now, we can hopefully agree that rules have an uncanny ability to help us determine our priorities.

The next lesson I had to learn about the nature of rules is that a rule must never be kept for the sake of keeping it. Nor should it be broken out of spite, especially when there's a perfectly good ego to break in its stead. By this I mean that our priority for keeping a rule should not be mere blind obedience, nor should it be arrogantly disregarded. A rule is established for an explicit purpose, be it our protection or some other benefit. Due to the autonomy permitted us by our free will, we get to participate in upholding that purpose or to trample it beneath our feet.

With these lessons in mind, we can explore the mysterious relationship between liberty and control. On the surface, the two seem to contradict one another, but I'm learning that they're actually quite dependent on each other. Nonetheless, there's a natural tension that arises out of their relationship, and we'd do well to press into it.

Until recently, I believed freedom meant being able to do whatever I want, whenever I felt like it. Control meant being able to manipulate my circumstances in order to get something I felt I needed for my fulfillment. What I didn't understand was that my false sense of freedom robbed me of my ability to choose, and my need to control my surroundings enslaved me to an entire world of responsibility that I was never meant to endure.

Yes, we do have free will, but that argument neglects the fact that our minds are broken, cursed, and hardly equipped for the task at hand—namely to find our way through this present darkness. Don't forget that we were designed for a Master long before we neglected Him, and the curse we've fallen under only further deceives us from the reality of our relationship with Him.

I came to this understanding largely because this so-called freedom that I relished for much of my life had become burdensome. It was heavy. Exhausting. Later, it became crippling. Those are not words we often hear people describe freedom. What had I been missing?

"Come to me, all who labor and are heavy laden, and I will give you rest. Take my yoke upon you, and learn from me, for I am gentle and lowly in heart, and you will find rest for your souls. For my yoke is easy, and my burden is light."
— Matthew 11:28-30

WHILE RECOVERING FROM MY ACCIDENT, I got to talk to Jesus about my misunderstanding of free will. In believing that my freedom permits me to do as I want, that is, as my flesh desires, I proceeded under the compulsions of that flesh. And we know that the flesh and the Spirit are at war within our hearts. I was bound—a slave to sin.

Jesus! I'd cry in despair (this was before the time in the pasture when Jesus's love descended from my mind and penetrated my heart). *I'm trapped. You know I want to do good, but every attempt to do so is a failure of epic proportions, and with every failure I feel like I'm moving further and further away from you. Why does this keep happening?*

In the following months, as the knowledge of His love became a reality I was experiencing in my heart, He showed me that I was, in fact, in bondage to my own freedom. As Jesus called me deeper into that space, He continued to reveal that my false sense of freedom was born out of my false sense of control.

Recall the time on the lake when I started using tobacco. I was angry that my mom was trying to control me. It was then and there that I adopted the mentality that whenever something was not going the way I wanted it to, I would turn to substance to return the element of control into my hands. As if to say, *"I don't like that my mom is trying to control me; I'm going to take matters into my own hands and make myself feel better by doing something she can't control."*

The Thrill of the Hunt

> In an act of arrogant defiance, I unknowingly traded in blind obedience for willful bondage, and bondage is simply not something God can bear to allow to come between Himself and His children.

I DON'T KNOW ABOUT YOU, but I've never met someone who didn't wish to live a life free of pain. Think about the happenings of any given day. By the time we've had breakfast, we've probably already complained about one thing or another a half-dozen times. Have you ever noticed how that seems to set the tone for the rest of the day?

It's quite natural to wish away pain. As we discussed earlier, anxiety comes from the vain attempt to avoid it. After all, we were never designed to experience any of it. But if we humbly acknowledge that pain is a reality of life under the curse of sin, we are invited to adopt a new perspective toward the purpose it serves in our lives.

In C. S. Lewis's exploration of *The Problem of Pain*, he opens the book by addressing the nature of God, and his first chapter points out God's Divine omnipotence. His next chapter portrays another divine characteristic embedded within the mystery of God—His divine goodness. As we're taught here in the Bible Belt, God's omnipotence is a given. He created the universe, so obviously He's all-powerful. But His goodness—now that is a truth much more difficult for us to stomach. If God is really all-good, why is pain woven into the fabric of our human dilemma? I'm sure you've heard someone pose the question, "If God is truly all-powerful and also all-good, why does He allow terrible things to happen?" In short, "Why does He allow pain?"

C. S. Lewis spent much of the first part of his life making that very argument. He was a devout (and angry) atheist and, ironically, he met Jesus after exhausting every attempt to disprove God's divine goodness.

It's safe to assume we're all familiar with Jeremiah's vision, illustrating God as the Potter and we are the clay, yet we might be tempted to attribute our likeness to clay as being something of little value. But this would be a grave misunderstanding of what Jeremiah was reveling in.

Lewis writes:

> "We are, not metaphorically but in very truth, a Divine work of art, something that God is making, and therefore something with which He will not be satisfied until it has a certain character. Here again we come up against what I have called an "intolerable compliment" . . . It is natural for us to wish that God had designed for us a less-glorious and less-arduous destiny; but then we are wishing not for more love but for less." [1]

If we come to accept that God, out of His Divine Goodness, is making us into a Divine work of art, then we must, too, accept the process through which God fashions us into a certain character. That artful process is Love, and who are we to question the tools at the Artist's disposal?

Here is where Lewis's exploration of pain more clearly aligns with our canine conversation:

> "[Love's] great merit lies in the fact that the association of (say) man and dog is primarily for the man's sake: he tames the dog primarily that he may love it, not that it may love him and that it may serve him, not that he may serve it . . . In its state of nature it has a smell, and habits, which *frustrate* man's love: he washes it, house-trains it, teaches it not to steal, and is so enabled to love it completely. To the puppy the whole proceeding world would seem, if it were a theologian, to cast grave doubts

on the 'goodness' of man: but the full-grown and full-trained dog, larger, healthier, and longer-lived than the wild dog, and admitted, as it were by Grace, to a whole world of affections, loyalties, interests, and comforts entirely beyond its animal destiny, would have no such doubts."[2]

Lewis goes on to make the fascinating claim that we may wish we were of less importance to God, that He would simply leave us to our natural impulses, that He would not painstakingly house-train or bathe us. But in such case, we would be desiring not more love, but far less.

If we agree with this account, why do we wish our pain away if it is the very thing which produces the fullness of life? Why do we devoutly claim to desire God's love and affection, yet cringe when the brush is applied to color our blank canvas? If we reject the process, we reject the Artist and find ourselves to be a clump of mud circling endlessly around the Potter's wheel. Only when we resolve to be fashioned into the very vessel that God longs to pour His Spirit into, shall we be set free of this cage of depravity.

Later in the chapter, Lewis suggests:

"When we want to be something other than the thing God wants us to be, we must be wanting what, in fact, will not make us happy. . . . God gives us what He has, not what He has not; He gives the happiness that there is, not the happiness that is not. To be God—to be like God and to share His goodness in creaturely response—to be miserable—these are the only three alternatives. If we will not learn to eat the only food that the universe grows—the only food that any possible universe can ever grow—then we must starve eternally."[3]

I don't know about you, but I spend a massive amount of time thinking about what I want. I can rarely, if ever, put my finger on it, and my mind is usually drawn to the things that are keeping me from getting there rather than the goal itself. With such a limited view, how could we ever know what we truly want? Do we ever consider the possibility that we want far less than what God wants to give us?

That's the entire point of *The Lord of the Rings,* authored by Lewis's good friend J. R. Tolkien. The cave dweller, Gollom, had stumbled upon a ring that wielded immense power. Gollom became consumed by its allure and retreated underground to simply stare at it and stroke it all day. It became his entire world and eventually cost him everything, all because he would not turn away and *remember* there is an entire universe beyond the cave in which he had confined himself. Opening his fist and shifting his gaze would have set his life on a completely different trajectory, one that might have led him back to the happiness and lightheartedness of his youth in the Shire. In fact, there is a moment where our protagonist recalls Gollom's true name—Sméagol—and a tension arises within Gollom where he faintly remembers a life before the curse of the ring. But, in the end, its allure ultimately becomes too powerful, and he pursues it into a volcanic lake.

Lewis and Tolkien were onto something, here, and, boy, would I have loved to listen in on one of their conversations. Surely, God gives to us out of the overflow of his happiness. He adorns every aspect of our lives with His Divine Goodness, regardless of whether we perceive it to be good. The more we loosen our grip on the false selves we've become fixated upon, the more we're able to receive of that overflow. And I believe both Lewis and Tolkien would agree that boundaries are, without a doubt, for our good, enabling us to more fully and rightly receive His Divine Goodness.

"Much of your pain is self-chosen. It is the bitter potion by which the physician within you heals your sick self. Therefore, trust the physician, and drink his remedy in silence and tranquility. For his hand, though heavy and hard, is guided by the hand of the Unseen. And the cup he brings, though it burns your lips, has been fashioned of the clay which the Potter has moistened with his own sacred tears." [4]

— Kahlil Gibran, author and poet

Yonah and a very stoic stone wall.

The Freedom of Boundaries

Yonah and I have been spending an awful lot of time in cemeteries lately. It's not a likely place for two adventurous creatures to seek out discovery. But, out of necessity, I stopped off at Old Gray Cemetery one wintery day when I didn't have time to take Yonah to the dog park.

Life has a funny way of insisting itself upon us. As our minds and bodies have a natural tendency to grow old and stagnant, life springs forth from a frosted, barren ground to remind us there is always newness to behold.

During our first visit at the cemetery, Yonah quickly darted off and left me to my own wandering. I meandered around the cemetery reading the dedication plaques and noting the dates of the nineteenth-century gravestones.

To my intrigue, Old Gray was not named after its drab, stoic appearance; instead, it received its title in honor of the English poet, Thomas Gray. I'd never heard of him and became curious what his connection with Knoxville was. I didn't find one, but I did, however, discover that he is renowned as one of England's most famous poets. What's even more interesting (and relative to our conversation) is that he had only thirteen poems published and at least one cemetery to commemorate his name at the time of his death. Talk about a guy who struggled with identity and control!

A waist-high stone wall encircles the thirteen-acre plot. An ironically broken-down fountain is situated on a central hill overlooking the ominous scene. Standing next to the fountain (at least in the dead of winter), I have a pretty clear view of Yonah no matter where he is in the cemetery. Thankfully, I noticed there's only one entrance to keep an eye on. Less thankfully, that exit happens to face the highly trafficked street.

What I didn't expect to find in this seemingly lifeless scenario was a bustling ecology of squirrels and birds that would give Seven Islands Bird Sanctuary a run for its money. Yonah was determined to introduce himself to each and every one of them by name, and he wasted little time doing so.

As I watched Yonah roam, I cautiously eyed the Broadway exit, knowing if he were to venture out of the wrought-iron gates, he would most certainly be killed in traffic. It would make sense for me to post up by the exit and confidently guard Yonah from leaving the cemetery. But to do so would limit my ability to share in his joyous escapade.

I resolved to linger next to the central fountain and catch glimpses of the brown flashes of Yonah darting among the graves, chasing the critters up the trees. I began to wonder what exactly it was about this graveyard that was so captivating to both Yonah and myself.

In 2011, I spent a few months visiting a friend in Paris. As we explored the city together, she took me to the famous P'ere Lachaise cemetery in the northeast part of the city. Coincidentally, P'ere Lachaise was the inspiration for Old Gray Cemetery, which seems weird to think about one cemetery inspiring another. Regardless, it was the first time I'd ever been awestruck by the beauty of a cemetery. I remember being fascinated that the sole purpose of a cemetery is to house the dead, yet these tombstones were masterfully and elaborately crafted. So much beauty for a such a lifeless place. It's curious why someone would want to have such an absurdly large tombstone to house their five-foot body. (I've never been to the pyramids in Egypt, but I imagine I'd be even more perplexed.) These people were no longer able to tell their story; perhaps they hoped their tombstone would do the talking for them.

There in Old Gray, I wondered what its inhabitants would say of their lives back in the eighteenth and nineteenth centuries, and my mind revisited many of the same questions it asked several years earlier.

Did these people's lives go the way they'd hoped? Did they find all they sought, and did their toiling fill the desires of their heart? What would they tell us about the long-forgotten lessons they learned before their bodies were laid to rest and their mouths sealed with a gravestone? Am I in danger of making those same empty mistakes that cause so many to trudge through this world already dead to the life around them?

It was the strangest feeling, as if I were stuck in some time warp and taken back to P'ere Lachaise. And without Yonah's unparalleled excitement to juxtapose the morbid thought, I might have once again missed what Jesus was trying to show me. No matter how hard we try to resist it, no matter how distracted we make ourselves to ignore the thought, our bodies are all going straight to the ground.

We can choose to spend our time in such vain ways that all we leave behind is an elaborate tombstone in a fancy cemetery such as P'ere Lachaise. Or we can remember that our lives already hold infinite value because we are formed in the likeness of God Himself. Living from this reality, we might stop striving so hard to be who we already are—fully loved, fully accepted sons and daughters of the Living God.

With these revelations now rousing my sleepy heart, my body had a new life to it that it could hardly contain. I wanted to run through the cemetery with the same vigor as Yonah, with the same vibrance as Mary Magdalene after Jesus appeared to her in the garden. She rushed back to the disciples, who, at the time, were in hiding, heartbroken, and afraid for their lives. We discussed this earlier when Jesus was preparing His disciples for the onset of their great commission.

"Behold, the hour is coming, indeed it has come, when you will be scattered, each to his own home, and you will leave me

alone. Yet I am not alone, for the Father is with me. I have said these things to you, that in me, you may have peace. In the world you will have tribulations (frustrations). But take heart; I have overcome the world."

— John 16:32-33

The disciples were, in a sense, training from the very first moment Jesus called them to follow Him. But because they could not see that this was all part of their training, the disciples went into hiding, just as Jesus predicted. They were scattered, each to their own home, just as we all are. But with the good news that Mary carried into their hiding place, the veil was lifted.

Imagine the revelation that was right before them the entire time they had been walking with Jesus! Jesus was who He said He was; they simply didn't have the eyes to see it. Their minds had to be transformed. When Mary burst through the doors of their hideout and shared what the angel had told her, the reality of Jesus's kingdom came crashing through the stratosphere of their minds and penetrated their hearts; in that moment, everything was different. That was, in truth, their invitation to begin a rigorous transformation of the mind.

I imagined them thinking to themselves, *Wait, Jesus said He was going to overthrow the rulers of the world, then the rulers of the world killed Him, but now He's alive? Obviously, He is who He said He was, so what does that mean about all the other stuff He said?*

My thoughts were shattered as I noticed Yonah nearing the entrance. From where I stood in the center, it was more than 150 yards away; if he got the wild hair to explore beyond the walls that could keep him safe, there was little I could do to stop him. Thankfully, he passed by the threshold, either unaware of or uninterested in what was outside. He was content to remain within the safety of its walls, and I couldn't help but wonder why so much of my life has been the complete opposite.

I can say for certain that it wasn't out of willful obedience that Yonah minded the boundaries; he was simply enthralled with the adventure before him. His master was inside, along with plenty of birds and squirrels to chase to his heart's content. I, on the other hand, have a tendency to entertain the thought of what adventures the outside world can offer. And Jesus, in His Divine omnipotence, has every ability and right to guard the threshold and ensure my safety. Out of His Divine Goodness and Love, He chooses not to, and it must pain Him so to watch myself and so many others venture out into a world which we were not made to inhabit.

Of course, Jesus's vision is not limited to the space within the worldly cemetery in which I so often find myself. Like the good Father He is, He lets me roam in search of greener pastures, knowing that what I seek cannot be found outside of these boundaries He has drawn for my safety. He patiently waits in the center of the Garden, longing for me to return to His side and simply lie at His feet, knowing the rest it brings to my weary soul. In those moments of rebellion, I inevitably find myself in danger. He hears my cry for help and goes in search of my heart, finding me ensnared in the thorns of my sin.

He frees me from my entrapment, takes me upon His shoulders, and carries me back to the Garden for which I was made. On the way home, instead of lecturing me about my stupidity, He whispers His love into my longing ears and quiets my fearful heart. He lays me down beside the cool waters of His (unbroken) fountain, and it's there that I find the rest I so restlessly seek apart from him.

The Thrill of the Hunt

"The Philosopher and the Cobbler" (Kahlil Gibran)

> "There came to a cobbler's shop a philosopher with worn shoes. And the philosopher said to the cobbler, 'Please mend my shoes.'
>
> "And the cobbler said, 'I am mending another man's shoes now, and there are still other shoes to patch before I can come to yours. But leave your shoes here, and wear this other pair today; and tomorrow come for your own.'
>
> "Then the philosopher was indignant, and he said, 'I wear no shoes that are not my own.'
>
> "And the cobbler said, 'Well then, are you in truth a philosopher, and cannot enfold your feet with the shoes of another man? Upon this very street there is another cobbler who understands philosophers better than I do. Go to him for your mending.'[5]

This season of life can be summed up with a single word—*healing*. As this inevitably comes up in a multitude of conversations, friends often ask me to expand upon what I mean by that.

"What specifically are you being healed from?" they implore, recognizing the smile on my face goes far beyond the physical healing that has taken place since my accident. While no less miraculous, it has been, at the very least, a catalyst to the transformation of my heart, and with the transformation of heart comes the transformation of sight.

When I attempt to explain, I hardly know where to begin. With my physical healing, it's much easier to point out the injury that nearly left me paralyzed. We can understand after an incident like that, a broken body naturally begins to heal itself to the best of its abilities. But with matters of a healing heart, it can be difficult to pinpoint the source of so many of wounds I didn't even know existed.

While the wounds themselves are incredibly elusive, the symptoms are ever-present. For years I've been bewildered by these symptoms, wondering why I can't will them away. They're caused by sin, right? Shouldn't I just be able to stop sinning?

Well, by now I shouldn't have to tell you that hasn't worked out so well for me. Every attempt to free myself from the strongholds of sin has laughably fizzled out within a few short weeks, leaving me more despairing than ever. So how does this change occur, and where do I find the healing I so desperately long for?

Along the way, I spoke to countless pastors, mentors, and friends, only to walk away from those conversations wondering if I had some undiagnosable (and certainly incurable) disease. I suffered depression, bitterness, and even suicidal thoughts, wondering what it would take to bring about the change I knew I wanted. In that timeless season of hopeless outrage, my mind exhausted itself with the single question—*Jesus, what's wrong with me?*

"Now there is in Jerusalem by the sheep gate a pool, called 'Bethesda' (meaning house of mercy), having five porticoes. In these lay a multitude of those who were sick, blind, lame, and withered [waiting for the moving of the waters]; for an angel of the Lord went down at certain seasons into the pool and stirred up the water; whoever then first, after the stirring up of the water, stepped in was made well from whatever disease with which he was afflicted. A man was there who had been ill for thirty-eight years. When Jesus saw him lying there, and knew he had already been a long time in that condition, He said to him, 'Do you wish to get well?' The sick man answered

him, 'Sir, I have no man to put me into the pool when the
water is stirred up, but while I am coming, another steps
down before me.' Jesus said to him, 'Get up, pick up your mat
and walk.' Immediately, the man became well and picked up
his mat and began to walk."

— John 5:2-8, 13

Like most of us who've grown up in the Bible Belt, I've heard
this story a thousand times. I used to skim past it like I did
with so many other stories. On the surface, it's not that cli-
mactic. In my mind, there's a bunch of sick people hanging
by the pool. Jesus walks past and realizes He hasn't healed
anybody yet that day, so He steps up to the first guy he sees,
asks him an obvious question, then tells him to get up and
go home. Pretty standard stuff for Jesus, right? Or maybe He
wants to show all the sick people that healing doesn't come
from the stirring waters and that it comes from God, which
is true, except it completely glosses over the profundity of
what's actually taking place in this story.

Thankfully, I've had a couple mentors call out the beautiful intricacies of why John chose this story in particular to
be a part of his gospel. After the incident that nearly left me
paralyzed, my eyes were opened to the reality that I am
counted among those waiting by the pool for any chance of
healing.

From this new perspective, I can envision Jesus making
His way through the crowd. Each person there was suffering
from one illness or another. Regardless of the degrees of their
suffering, they share an equal desire to be made well. They
long to return to normal functionality, and maybe if they're
healed, there's a chance they'll be reaccepted into their society. For those who have always been cast out, maybe they
could experience acceptance for the first time in their lives.

Because of their pain and frustration, it's doubtful they were waiting around in silence like a Tibetan monastery until the waters stirred. Their desire for healing was urgent; therefore, we can imagine it was a pretty chaotic place. Perhaps they were comparing their illnesses and suggesting who was more qualified for urgent healing (which would be all too fitting for our day, as well).

In any event, Jesus singled out this crippled man out and approached him without drawing any attention to what was about to take place. I wonder why He chose this man to ask the obvious question. Did this man have more faith than the rest of the crowd?

Judging by his answer, I think not. When Jesus asked him if he wished to be well, the man immediately spouted off an excuse for why he was unable to enter the pool. While he was, in fact, explaining the rather obvious reason why he couldn't enter the pool, he completely missed the question (largely because he didn't know who was asking). His response does, however, say far more than he could have imagined.

His response revealed three things. First, he acknowledged that he was, in fact, unwell. Also, that he had tried repeatedly to enter the pool and was unable to do so *on his own*. Finally, he claimed that he had yet to meet someone who was willing to help him. Everyone else was so concerned about their own well-being (or lack thereof) that no one would help him enter the pool. Thus, he was left to wait for thirty-eight years.

Day after day, year after year, he lay there on his mat, hoping for his big break. Then, up walks a man who asks him a very simple question. It might have been an obvious question, but one the man had likely never been asked. The urgency of his reply seems to indicate his frustration with his repeated efforts and helplessness with which he was now faced.

"Do you want to be well?" Jesus asks.

"Look, man, whoever you are, I've tried over, and over, and over again. Every chance I get, someone beats me to it. No one will help me, and as much as I'd like to, I clearly cannot do it on my own."

Without hesitation, Jesus invited him to stand up, to do something he'd never done before and had no reason to believe would ever be a part of his reality. Honestly, can you imagine what was going through this guy's mind?

Seriously, stop and think about this.

In the eternal moment between Jesus's question and the invalid's response, surely his world came to an abrupt halt. By John's account, there is no indication that the chaos surrounding their interaction was suddenly stilled. Jesus didn't quiet the noise of the crowd in anticipation of his answer.

Yet the question remained—*"Do you want to be healed?"*

Still, the man could have hesitated, and perhaps he did, if only in his mind. But Jesus's simple question required a simple answer, and the way he chose to respond altered the rest of his life.

The man stood to his feet. In responding to Jesus's call, he miraculously found that the strength he'd never experienced was suddenly provided for him.

But Jesus didn't just tell him to get up, walk away, forget his past, and to go forth rejoicing in his newfound freedom. Jesus told him to rise and take his mat with him. This guy had been glued to his mat for his entire life, and the first opportunity he had to leave it behind was met with an invitation to carry it with him.

Who is this Jesus that would ask such a seemingly obvious question, and why on earth would Jesus insist that he take the mat with him? If there was anything that the man had grown to resent beyond the people around him unwilling to help him into the healing waters, surely it was the filthy mat he'd been bound to from birth.

The moment the man stood to his feet, he found that the provision he'd been waiting for was now standing right there in front of him. The mat that symbolized all that the world rejected about him was instantly the lightest thing he'd ever carried in his life.

IN THE PASTURE THAT DAY, my mind had long since convinced itself that it needed my ex-fiancée, or anyone else for that matter, to affirm the security and well-being of my personhood. While Jesus was showing me an ocean, I was thinking about the tear rolling down my cheek.

Jesus compassionately asked me in the midst of my pain, *"Child, why are you crying?"*

When I whimpered, *"She doesn't love me,"* I was at the same time admitting that I longed for love. Like the lame man, I was unable to help myself and yearned for an acceptance that could make me feel whole. All my life I had yet to encounter such a love, mainly because I had a very finite idea of what that was supposed to look like.

In response, Jesus insisted, *"Perhaps not, but I love you."*

Even still, I was filled with sadness. In truth, it wasn't the loss of her love that I lamented; I was afraid of what that loss could mean—that I was unlovable. I was essentially saying, *"If the one person whom I thought I could count on to love me, no matter what happens, doesn't love me, then no one does,"* which is an incredibly unfair burden to place on any broken human's shoulders. I thought I knew where to seek and find the love, and once found, it would instill the behavioral changes I desired—the changes that would earn

God's acceptance I so desperately needed. I later came to find out that the motives behind those changes were still a striving for that same acceptance. I was trying to perform in a way where Jesus would be pleased with me, and I could earn His grace in good conscience. In doing so, I repeatedly missed the mystery of the revelation that had been standing before me the whole time.

We'll talk more about those motives later on, but after all those years of obsessing over the symptoms of my broken humanity and seeking an answer I thought my eyes would certainly recognize, Jesus responded with a question of his own: *"Would you believe me if I told you that I am enough for you in this place in your heart?"*

I didn't know how to respond. I probably had the same look on my face that the lame man had when Jesus asked him if wanted to be well. No one had ever asked me that question before. I'd forced that burden upon dozens of people but it had never been voluntarily assumed.

While I certainly could not accept in that moment that Jesus's love was enough to fill all the empty places of my shattered heart, I could admit for the first time in my life that this level of acceptance was all I'd ever truly wanted—just one person to tell me I meant the world to them.

I'm not saying that my entire life now made sense, because it didn't. I still had (and have) so many questions, but I no longer insisted upon an answer. Every tension I sought to escape through relationships and substance abuse, every anxiety that I desired relief from, was a yearning for security, for acceptance, for significance. I needed to know that I was safe. I longed to believe that I was worthy of love. I searched the world over to give me something it was never intended to offer, and I found myself wanting.

The world led me to believe that if I worked hard enough, I could break through the boundaries that were keeping me from where I wanted to be. After lying by the pool of 'Mercy' for twenty-eight years wondering why no one would help me into the waters, I came to the end of myself and encountered a Jesus who had been waiting for me every single moment of my life.

Let there be no mistake—twenty-eight years of looking to a dead world to give me life had done a hell of a lot of damage. I had been chewed up, spit out, and left for dead when Jesus found me. But when He looked at me with those compassionate eyes, empathetic because He too felt the sting of rejection from anyone who ever has or ever will live, I knew beyond a shadow of a doubt that this was real Love. Something magnificent happened that day. The Jesus I'd only heard about asked if He could come stay in my home.

He invited me to talk about all that I was ashamed of, all the ugliness I'd come to believe about myself. This was the mat I'd been lying on my whole life, waiting to be made well. Ironically, I now walked with a limp and my body was covered in the scars of past wounds. To my wildest surprise, He wasn't ashamed of them; in fact, they were His great joy.

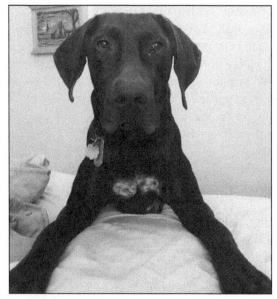

Yonah propped up on my bed. "So, what's next?"

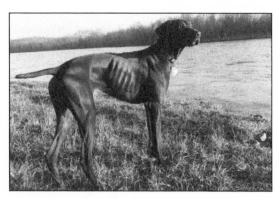

Yonah on river's edge, checking out the action.

7

The Joy of the Master

"The glory of God is Man fully alive."

— Saint Irenaeus

*"The only true self-fulfillment—if we must use such a term—
is to be sought in obedience to the lordship of, and commun-
ion with, the living Christ. Genuine fulfillment of self is
expressed in forgetfulness of self and in the love of others ex-
emplified by the Savior of the world."*

— Patrick Henry Reardon

FROM AN OUTSIDER'S PERSPECTIVE, one might imagine Yonah's training to be complete. He goes everywhere with me. He minds (most days), and we have a bond that's undeniable to anyone who bears witness. Everywhere we go together, I'm always conscious of where he is. If I step out of the room for a moment, friends often tell me he scanned the room the entire time I was away.

Passersby frequently compliment how well he listens. I assure them it's entirely Yonah's disposition and that I simply got lucky with such a great dog. While that is true, it completely disregards the countless hours we have spent to get to where we are.

Of course, it's always nice to know people have taken notice of our training efforts. But it's indescribably more fulfilling to live out the joy of being master and provider to such a lovable and loving creature. In fact, now that we enjoy such a full and rich bond, the memory of the many hardships of training has all but faded.

Recall C. S. Lewis's insight that man disciplines a dog to make it more lovable than it would be in its wild, natural state. He imagines that the entire training process would seem, at first, to make the puppy doubt the 'goodness' of its master. But in submitting to discipline, the puppy's life is opened up to a whole world of affections, loyalties, interests, and comforts entirely beyond its animal destiny to the extent that the well-trained dog would have no such doubts about its master's good intentions.

"It will be noted that the man takes all the pains with the dog, and gives all these pains to the dog. . . . because it is so nearly lovable that is worth his while to make it fully lovable."[1]

What a beautiful illustration of the relational dynamic we have with our Heavenly Father, our eternally Good Master! Jesus underwent an unimaginable extent of pain so that we may enter into the fullness of His life, and yet even after all of that, His love for us still affords us the choice to respond or not. By his blood we were purchased. By all cosmic and supernatural accounts, we are His. Still, He never demands our obedience, nor does He ever renounce His invitation to follow and trust. He simply is the fullness, and He invites us to come and have our fill.

So, what does Lewis mean that we're nearly lovable? Hopefully, by now, we're in agreement that we cannot earn God's love; therefore, how can we be so nearly lovable that God strives to make us fully lovable? The Bible claims that we were a dream in the mind of God long before the foundation of the earth was lain. Did He stop just short of His goal and figure He'd pick it up on a rainy day? How does that align with our understanding of training and the way we measure it in terms of progress?

I SPENT SO MANY YEARS believing in the illusion of progress, that self-fulfillment could be found by doing some great work for God that would bring glory to His name. From this perspective, my joy was something to be experienced in the future and was, therefore, always eluding me. I was focused on the work rather than the glory of God. I wanted to glorify myself and claim I was doing it in Jesus's name. In doing so, I missed the very source of Life that I was yearning to achieve. It's no wonder that I did neither.

As I continued in this Pharisaic cycle, my life riddled with sin (not the least of which was self-absorption), I felt I was somehow failing him, that He was disappointed with me, and that I had a very specific amount of time to clean up my act before my ticket was called and I missed my chance at eternity.

My friends, I can hardly express the sense of relief that came from finding that this was simply not the case! If I was able to clean up my act, I would have done it by now, but that was about as successful as Yonah willing himself into human form. I promise I've tried everything imaginable outside of donning the cloth and joining a monastery. If we were able to will ourselves into fulfillment, there would have been no need for Jesus to don flesh and join in the pain of living under the curse of man.

And that fulfilled future I yearned for so badly, I'm pleased to announce, is not out there. It's right here, today in this very moment. And all God wants from us and for us is to simply be what He made us to be—His children.

When we try to be something other than what He dreamed up before time began, we neglect our very nature and simultaneously accuse God of flawed design. Unlike Lewis's illustration of a dog being so nearly lovable that it is worth our time to make him fully lovable, as God's children, we are already fully lovable. And guess what? It's not because of anything we ever did or ever could do. It is simply and magnificently the reality of Divine Goodness manifested in the life, death, and resurrection of Jesus Christ.

This same Jesus who entered into our suffering also shares all He has with all those He loves, namely His fullness, which means our fullness is found in the living Christ alone. This simple truth wonderfully undoes everything we think we know about progress. To *become* (tracing the word back to its origin) means 'to come to a place' or 'to receive.' In this sense, I wonder what is to become of us if we have already arrived.

As we are so often tempted to doubt in the Goodness, we'd do well to remember what Lewis wrote. God can only give to us of what He has. He cannot give to us what He has not. And if God only has happiness and fullness of life, then we cannot receive anything beyond that (as if that couldn't be enough). To be God, to be like God and participate with Him for the life of the world, or to be miserable—these are our only three alternatives.

We saw what happened to Adam and Eve when they believed they could attain God's nature, and we don't have to look very far to find someone who's up to their neck in misery. In fact, some of us don't have to look further than our own noses. I don't know about you, but I want to see what's behind Door No. 2. I want to experience the fullness Jesus spoke of when He said, *"I came to give life, and life to the fullest."* And if Jesus came to give us joy in the present moment, perhaps we should spend less time grasping for it and more time with our hands and hearts open to receive.

I know I'm not alone in this. No one wants to be 'nearly lovable,' nor do they want to be 'partly alive.' Yet who among us feels they are fully alive? How many of us exhaust ourselves trying to bridge the gap between 'nearly' and 'fully'?

Jesus didn't say, *"Come to me when you have it all figured out and you're not an absolute mess."* He says, *"Come to me all who are weary, and I will give you rest."* That's some good news. We were not made for striving; we were made for living. It's the Father's job to make us whole and, my dear friends, the job is done. Come as you are.

If we can't be more fully alive, the Father's work then becomes removing the obstacles that keep us from believing that. For that process to start, we have to be open to what the Father is showing us, and we have to be honest about whether that's something that truly hinders our ability to live life with open hands. After all, if our hands are full, we can't receive anything. If they are open, we may receive all things.

I THINK OFTEN ABOUT THIS concept of living life with open hands. We have such a tendency to hold on to things tightly, whether it's some future version of ourselves or an ideal outcome of some event. It echoes our previous discussion of expectations and our insistence on being in the driver's seat.

Whatever the object of our imagination, we attach ourselves to it, and the slightest threat of separation or disturbance is enough to turn many of us into primal savages. At best, we complain in a subconscious and pathetic attempt to tip the scales back in our favor. At worst, we suffer a mental breakdown that brings everything about our identity into question. Don't believe me? Try telling a sixteen-year-old they're not an adult. Try telling someone with early signs of dementia that you've noticed their symptoms. We react this way to an attack on our ego because it shakes us to our core and dismantles our entire interior universe.

Humor me for a moment, but let's apply this to Yonah's world. What would happen if I told him all the birds and squirrels were no longer in existence? Can you comprehend the level of anxiety that would produce in his life? For Yonah, birds and squirrels are *everything*. He devoutly believes his mission on earth is to pursue any and all winged and bushy tailed creatures. If they all vanished, he would be devastated and find himself without a purpose.

As humans, we do the same thing. Does this indicate a design flaw in our nature? I think not. We were designed for attachment, which in turn calls into question the nature of the various things to which we attach ourselves. The problem, or rather, the tension, arises when we insist that those things are able to fulfill us, and yet they always fall short of that goal. If we accept the reality that they cannot satisfy our deepest longing means that our time and efforts pursuing them have been wasted. Without their false promise of fulfillment, our lives appear to be meaningless.

If, instead, we come to believe and see that the flaw is not in desire itself, but rather, in the various things we desire, how would that impact our dependence and insistence on them?

These desires in and of themselves aren't necessarily wrong; it's that the objects of those desires simply don't have the capacity to sustain the sort of longing God intentionally placed into our hearts. That's why we insist on needing more of the same thing, or we just walk away and find some new object of our desire to devote ourselves to. As such, these things distract us from our true identity as sons and daughters of God, and we go to person after person, place after place, thing after thing, always needing more, yet never having enough.

Still, there is a void in our hearts that we cannot deny. We recognize it because the desire never goes away. What could possibly satisfy that level of bottomless desire?

IF WE LOOK AROUND AT the various people we encounter throughout our days, our desires appear to be very different from one another. The businessman running down the crowded sidewalk is late for work, and he was hoping for a raise this month. The couple he bumps into outside the coffee shop is trying to enjoy the last morning of their anniversary. The owner of the coffee shop had another fight with his wife the night before and grossly mistreats the homeless man sitting at one of his bistro tables. The homeless man, of course, is simply trying to rest his feet after rummaging through restaurant dumpsters all night looking for something to eat.

It would seem these people have little in common except that their worlds collided for a brief moment outside this hypothetical coffee shop. But if we peel back the layers just a bit, we discover that deep down, they all want the security and peace that they believe will come with the gratification of those desires. Yes, they might experience security, joy, and peace for a moment, but just like the homeless man's basic desire for food, he couldn't possibly eat enough to satisfy his belly for the rest of the week. He'll spend the following night searching for another meal.

This example only scratches the surface of how our present desires point to something more internal. But if we have the courage to dig deeper, there's a wealth of joy and peace just waiting to be discovered, and there is much freedom in the unveiling of our deepest motives. The deeper we dig, the more riches we find. This, of course, is too great a task to do by ourselves and with our limited vision. We need help from someone more experienced in matters of the heart.

Fortunately, Jesus takes great joy in walking through those spaces and is eager to reveal the relentlessness of His pursuit. His life is the reality of this love, and my life is a testament to the fact that our God will not stand for His children to live in bondage. He has declared His victory over the power of sin and death, and He offers this love, along with His joy, freely to all who would come rest at the foot of His throne.

Religion is a barrier to all this freedom Jesus came to offer. For most of my life leading up to the accident, I suffered under the oppression of religion. Because my perspective of God was skewed, so, too, was my perspective of myself. I grew up believing that God was unable to be close to me when I disobediently walked in sin. But this could not be further from the truth and is the exact reason why Jesus adamantly opposes religion.

Religion is a manmade institution created to fix us, or at the very least, give us the illusion of control that keeps us from becoming worse. But God is not in the business of religion, nor is He interested in fixing us. As He does with all things, He wants to heal and make new all that has been broken and cursed. In my case, He has to undo all the things that religion had done, starting with the way I viewed myself. As He began to heal my heart and transform my eyes, He pointed out how much I hated myself for not being able to live up to the rules I thought I needed in order for God to approve of me. He graciously walked with me back to where I began believing in the lie that shame had spoken over me from a very early age.

It started to make sense why I was never able to will myself into perfection—to manipulate and polish my life in order to make myself presentable before a God who already adored me. God opened my eyes to the reality that until I am able to love and accept even the messiest parts of my life, I simply cannot allow even the God of the universe to love them, too.

I must admit the journey back through a lifetime of wounds has been far from comfortable. Unlike religion, which is very "cut and dried, don't do this, do that, then you'll be saved," this adventure with Jesus has completely debunked the myth of certainty. The ego is impressively elusive and often disguises itself as righteousness, which is, again, religion. But the mystery of God's love opens up more questions and reveals the motives behind our actions. This, of course, is a long and slow process, but it's the only way to freedom and peace, and if we're being honest, that's what we're all searching for anyway.

I implore you to invite God to take you on this journey. He greatly delights in revealing Himself in the instant the wounds took place and the false identities were reinforced. Every revelation of his faithfulness deepens our trust and lavishly enriches our ever-present moments. This is the story of my life leading up to the moment His faithfulness and love clashed with the shameful reality of my unfaithfulness, and the aftermath of that collision has forever altered the trajectory of my life.

UNLIKE YONAH, I WAS RAISED in a fundamentalist Christian home where I attended a private Christian school from kindergarten to eighth grade. It was there that I first encountered the 'love' of Jesus. From this perspective, I was a safe distance from the fires of hell, so long as I made good grades, wore my pants at least two inches above my butt crack, and didn't beat my brothers over the head with anything other than a Bible.

135

The Thrill of the Hunt

I mentioned how my family had an uncanny number of rules. These rules often resulted in my exclusion from activities with friends. My curfew was several hours earlier than theirs. My TV time was always regulated, even outside our home. I couldn't go to a friend's house without an adult there. Looking back, these were all good rules, and I completely understand why they were put in place. But at the time, all I knew was that my friends had a lot more freedom than I did, and I felt like I was somehow socially falling behind.

Religion also taught me the fruits of the Spirit—love, joy, peace, patience, kindness, gentleness, and self-control. I must have been about fourteen years old when I first realized I possessed none of these traits. I'd been through Christian school, my parents served over the kids' ministry at church *and* taught Sunday school for young, married couples. I had memorized the whole book of James (for two dollars a verse *Cha-ching!*) and didn't kiss a girl until freshman year of high school. Surely, I was a Christian, right?

So why wasn't I experiencing any of these delicious fruits I'd always heard about?

Like most other fourteen-year-old boys, I was confused, terrified, and subsequently angry as hell as I transitioned from a small, private Christian school to the most diverse public school in the city. As I attempted to retain the knowledge and preparation I had received in middle school, I quickly found the world wasn't quite as black and white as I had been led to believe.

Of course, I didn't realize any of this at the time. But as I look back, you could say I felt like I knew what the whole Jesus thing was about and it was clearly not working out the way I thought it was supposed to. In my limited experience, people who follow Jesus weren't supposed to have tension.

Out of those seeds of tension grew a shame that began to take root in every area of my life. I remember being quiet at home, mostly keeping to myself. When I was out in public and away from the standard of perfection I presumed I was being held to under my parent's roof, I was loud, goofy, and incredibly obnoxious.

I wanted to obey my parents and make them proud (and stay out of trouble), but I was also conflicted with my need for affirmation from my peers. I developed a performance-based mentality out of these juxtaposed personalities, and that conflict came to a head on the lake that day I started using tobacco, when I shrugged off the conscious desire to please my parents. Angrily, I stepped into any role that was required of me to bring about the illusion of acceptance. If that meant breaking a rule or two, so be it. As far as I was concerned, it was my parents' fault for setting those rules in the first place.

Throughout high school, my friends seemed comfortable and fearless, and I eagerly stepped into every opportunity to prove I was worthy of their acceptance. Little did I know they were all as hopelessly insecure as I was. Not surprisingly, whatever level of acceptance I was able to conjure up was far from adequate. As such, I wanted to get out of there as soon as possible and chose to graduate high school a semester early. At the time, I told myself I was eager to start college classes. But in truth, I was desperately embarrassed for never being able to secure the acceptance of my peers.

I didn't understand that my problems were not rooted in my behavior; they were rooted in my skewed perception of God. If our vision of God is skewed, then our vision of ourselves is also skewed. Religion taught me that God knows everything about me. Because I was keenly aware of my shortcomings underneath the laws of religion, I presumed

The Thrill of the Hunt

God was disappointed with me and was waiting for me to clean up my act before he delivered me from my shame. I unknowingly went in search for things to validate that story, that lie, I continued to believe.

As I went forth in the pursuit, always avoiding the ugliness of my life, that tendency for escape led me to join a fraternity in hopes that I might secure the acceptance of my friends from high school, the same ones I tried to impress with my tobacco, alcohol, and marijuana use.

Obviously, this didn't work out, so I again tried to escape, this time moving across the country to the allure of California. Because of the natural excitement that occurs when you leave the safety of the old world and enter the unknown, I believed I was getting closer to finding my true self.

Naturally, the allure of California eventually wore off and I moved back to Knoxville, though I returned with some sense of validation for having done something adventurous. After all, most of my high school friends had stayed in our hometown, a town I'd grown suspicious of having nothing to offer but boredom and repetition.

Those friends from my old life, along with the ones I gained upon my return, were eager to hear where my adventures had taken me, which fed into my twenty-year-old ego (you know, the one that makes you feel invincible). I had developed a reputation for being mysterious, a free spirit, and someone who I believed to be impervious to the emotions of everyday life.

I had no idea that my attachment to that illusion had gone far beyond merely seeking the approval of my peers. Substances such as alcohol and marijuana had now become my safety net. Any incident that encroached upon this illusion of being mysterious, a quick hit was more than enough to alleviate my fears. I was slowly killing my emotions, all in the attempt to reinforce my false identity.

As with any attachment, my tolerance grew and I needed more and more of these substances to accomplish the same level of numbness. It was no longer enough to have a few beers and call it a good night. It became about pushing the boundaries, if boundaries were to be perceived at all.

That's about the time I took my first job in the restaurant industry, where I met all sorts of colorful folks who introduced me to the world of psychedelics. At that point, life was all about having an experience—anything to further separate me from the awkward, sheltered self I'd grown to hate so much.

It's also important to note around this time I'd been reading a book called *The Shack*, which tells the story of a man's radical encounter with the Trinity. He's mysteriously invited up to a shack in the woods, where he meets various personalities of the triune God who want to talk to him about a burden he's been carrying for far too long. It's a beautiful illustration of the timeless nature of God and is understandably a very mystical story, where nothing is quite as it seems.

With this illustration fresh in my mind on one particular night, my friends and I planned on going to see a buddy's band play at a local venue. We wanted to ramp up the intensity of the show and decided to indulge in a moderate dosage of high-quality LSD.

I, of course, was never one to shy away from such an experience. I had partaken several times before and knew the dosage I was comfortable handling. As we sat back and waited for the ride to start, I caught one of my buddies dropping a few more doses in my beer. He had a deviant smile, to which I shrugged and figured, *"What the hell? Live a little."*

The Thrill of the Hunt

(I found out the next day his dosage had quadrupled my comfort level.)

Shortly after getting to the show, I quickly discovered what "*What the hell? Live a little.*" meant. What ensued was the unveiling of my eyes to a spiritual realm I can only describe as the underworld, and it was more terrifying than anything I had ever imagined.

If you know nothing else about psychedelics, know that the well-being of your experience is almost entirely up to your present mindset. If you enter that space feeling afraid, you're likely going to have a terrible time. If you step confidently, knowing everything that happens should be viewed through the filter of the drug, you can keep one foot in reality and the other is free to entertain this alternate universe you've chosen to dabble in.

Unfortunately, no one shared this insight with me beforehand. I confidently stepped into that space, only to quickly realize I wasn't as sure-footed as I'd led myself to believe. While I was waiting outside the venue, the drugs were taking their toll and things started to get a little blurry. I wasn't sure what was happening; all I knew was that things were getting intense. Every bit as frightening as the character's experience in *The Shack,* I could no longer discern what was real and what was in my mind.

I became paranoid that people were watching me, so I did what any twenty-one-year-old kid living that sort of lifestyle would do and lit up a cigarette. Jesus later showed me that this paranoia arose out of the shame and fear of condemnation I'd been avoiding my entire life. After all, I'd been living as if I had nothing to be ashamed of, nor to care about for that matter. But it was all a petty act of self-deception, and this was only the beginning of the Great Unravel.

Be cool. Be cool, I told myself.

It didn't work. I remember repeatedly asking my friends when the show was going to start so we could go inside. Jesus later pointed out that this was due to my tendency for escape. Whenever tension arises, stuff it back down, right? I was uncomfortable with my inability to control my surroundings, so I tried to manipulate my surroundings to regain the illusion of control. Minutes passed and I asked again and again. I eventually grew impatient and entered the venue by myself. Bad idea.

I descended into the venue, whose interior is themed as a grotto, or cave. I tried to just stand there and watch the current band perform, but the music (in my mind) started dragging along. Again, out of paranoia, I felt like the band was messing with me, mocking the negative energy I'd just brought into the venue. I imagined everyone was waiting for me to do something. I felt like I was supposed to be doing something to lift the energy of the place so the band would start playing normal again. I was conflicted about whether I should get on stage or not, and ultimately I recoiled in fear.

Jesus later explained that I'd done this out my need to perform for affirmation. Ever since middle school, maybe even earlier, I'd unknowingly felt like I had to step up in order to be noticed. But now I didn't want to be noticed. Now I was aware of my shame, my nakedness, and I retreated further into the venue.

I walked up to the water cooler and realized I had no idea how to operate it. I asked a couple of strangers if I could have some water. They pointed to the cooler and went on with their conversation. I admitted I could not figure out how to use it and asked if they would pour me some. Rightfully so, they looked at me like I was crazy and wandered off into the crowd. That's when I decided something was terribly wrong and I needed to get out of Dodge.

The Thrill of the Hunt

I ascended out of the grotto and back into the night. My house was only about a half-mile walk from the venue, but it might as well have been the distance from the Shire to Mordor, because if I couldn't operate a water cooler, there was not a chance I was going to be able to figure out how to get home. I began wandering through the market square outside of the venue. As I could no longer tell what was real and what my mind was projecting, this is when things started getting really scary.

I walked through the market and several people turned to mock me. I shrugged it off and acted like it didn't bother me, but I remember feeling so exposed, so hurt that they would go out of their way to make me feel the way I was feeling. All the tricks I'd used to cover up my nakedness, all the false identities I'd attached myself to in hopes of receiving their acceptance, were now on display for the world to view . . . and apparently to mock.

In that moment, I had quite literally never been further from knowing who I was. Fully exposed, I had nothing to cover my shame. Never have I been more terrified and alone.

Nearly a decade later, many of the details of what happened next are still vague. Amidst all the terrifying encounters, I begged for someone to help me understand what was happening. No one would answer. No one would really even allow me to stand by them. Even my girlfriend at the time continually eluded me whenever I approached her for help. I'd been blackballed, and who could blame them? I was a fraud.

Sometime later, I came to, lying on the dirty venue floor. The bass-heavy, spastic dubstep music (which by the way, I still firmly believe is from the devil himself) pulsed through my body, and a spotlight appeared in my mind's eye that left me paralyzed. To my horror, it grew larger and larger, and I couldn't escape it.

It turns out the infamous Trappist monk, Thomas Merton, had a similar vision around his twentieth year, though I believe neither hallucinogens nor dubstep were involved. I only include it here because he eloquently and precisely puts into words the hellish reality that we both experienced:

"I was overwhelmed with a sudden and profound insight into the misery and corruption of my own soul, and I was pierced deeply with a light that made me realize something of the condition I was in, and I was filled with horror at what I saw, and my whole being rose up in revolt against what was within me, and my soul desired escape and liberation and freedom from all this with an intensity and urgency unlike anything I had ever known before. And now I think for the first time in my whole life I really began to pray—praying not with my lips and with my intellect and my imagination, but praying out of the very roots of my life and of my being, and praying to the God I had never known, to reach down towards me out of His darkness and to help me to get free of the thousand terrible things that held my will in their slavery."[2]

In truth, that wasn't the first time I pleaded with God to take my life, but it was the first time I meant it. I asked Him to take or do whatever he wanted, as long as the nightmare ceased. All of a sudden, I had an overwhelming sense of urgency to rid myself of everything that I could be identified by—my I.D., wallet, cell phone. I even remember ripping my necklace off and tossing everything in the trash before wandering back out into the night.

I ached to go home; I wanted someone to help me understand what was happening, but I was trapped. I collapsed against the building outside with complete disregard as to what might become of me. I no longer cared if whoever I thought was looking for me found me. As far as I was concerned, nothing could be worse than what was already happening in my mind.

I have no idea how much time passed, but the next thing I remember is looking up to find a man parking his motorcycle a few yards away on the street. He dismounted and approached me ominously. He was dressed in all black and wore a full-faced helmet. His whole body was smoking through his clothes, and he just stood over me, glaring without lifting his tinted visor.

For whatever reason, I presumed he was one of the Four Horsemen Saint John described in his hellish vision known as Revelation. The rider didn't say anything, and I don't reckon I had much to say either. Believing him to be a part of whatever entity had been looking for me, I resolved that I'd been found. To be honest, I didn't care anymore, I just wanted it to be over and hoped they might have some answers whenever they decided to abduct me. He got back on his motorcycle and rode away.

The next thing I knew, I was wandering through a nearby parking lot. I was overwhelmingly relieved to find a friend had finally come to console me. I was weeping in despair, practically convulsing at this point, and I remember his stocky, tattooed forearm wrapped around my neck and pulled me close to him. *"I got you, homie. I got you,"* he repeated in my ear.

I don't entirely recall what happened next or how we got home that night, but I later found myself back at that friend's house in the early hours of the morning. The house was empty, and I asked him where everybody was.

"They gone, homie. It's all over. Just the people in this house is all that's left."

While his answer was fully intended to console me by saying the worst of the night was over, my chemically laced brain heard something completely different. I went to bed accepting the fact that I had died, and I was now in hell. I moped into the bedroom and tried to lay down, but my brain was so broken I couldn't even figure out how to lie in the bed properly. I remember the shame of trying to fall asleep, thinking *Man, it was right there all along. God gave me every opportunity to clean up my act, and I blew it.* I kept having this vision of the Underworld with endless columns of catacomb-like cells that were too short to fully stand up or lie down. I tried and tried to get comfortable but could find no rest. I didn't sleep a wink that night.

The next morning, I came back to reality (relatively speaking, of course). I was relieved to have somehow held onto my car keys through the nightmare, which was great news because I was supposed to be driving to Savannah, Georgia, that day to start school at my new university.

While it would be easy to write off the entire episode of my drug-induced vision as a stupid mistake, it was monumental to the lifelong story of Jesus rescuing from me from my bondage. That night I was shown, through a horror show of rejection, how lost I'd become in seeking the approval of others. For the first time in my life I was keenly aware of my complete lack of control and of how out of touch I was with my identity. When the time came to depend on my friends for help, the friends who I'd unknowingly depended on to tell me who I was, I was surprised to find them turning their back. After all, I'd subconsciously done everything for their approval. Why were they suddenly recanting their affirmation?

Deeply rooted beneath the rejection I experienced that night was the shame of being exposed as a fraud, and the paranoia that haunted me for years after the incident, sourced from my fear of condemnation. The God I grew up believing in would never stand for such foolishness and hypocrisy. He sent His Son to die for me, and I, apparently could not care less. I was appalled, although God revealed much later how differently He felt about the situation.

That night, Lucifer told me that I'd had the gift of God's sonship at my fingertips, only to throw it all way. He told me that everything was over, that all the good plans God had for me were voided by my negligence. In that moment, my drughazed, religion-filled mind believed it. I'll never forget the sadness and shame I felt as I resolved to sleep in hell that night, eternally separated from God. When I woke the next morning, the lie had planted a seed of self-loathing that quickly took root inside my heart. I was bound to that belief and convinced myself that I had failed my God and was unable to receive His love now.

I ARRIVED IN SAVANNAH, MY head still swimming with flashbacks of the hazy, drug-induced vision. I had so many questions about what had actually transpired that night, but the school year quickly started and it was all I could do to focus on the task at hand.

I wasn't entirely sure how I had ended up at this prestigious art school. To be honest, it was my dad's idea to send me there. He had always steered me in the right directions before, so I made up my mind to do whatever was necessary to get my degree in the most timely manner.

I had dabbled with art classes in high school, but I was a far cry from considering myself an artist. The talent I encountered with the 'real artists' in my classes was intimidating, and I once again found myself feeling like a fraud.

It's difficult to describe what happened over the next

several months. You have to understand that some part of me believed what I'd heard that night—*"It's over."* I thought that I was dead.

For the better part of a year, the hazy memories from my hellish vision continued to plague me, and I could no longer say for certain what was real and what was an illusion. Specific incidents would trigger those same fears, leading to insomnia and multiple panic attacks. I recall often lying awake through the night, terrified at the thought of opening my front door the following morning to learn that the Rapture had happened and I'd been left behind.

I was toeing the line of sanity, expecting that, at any moment, the curtain would be pulled back and all the actors of my present life would pop out of their hiding places, saying, *"Surprise! You're dead, dummy. Don't you remember? It's over. You had your chance and you blew it. You'd better get used to life in hell."*

I grew suspicious of the people around me. I tried to play it cool when I was out with friends, but the slightest occurrence might jog my memory and my anxiety would skyrocket. I raced home, closed every blind in the house, and cowered in the living room as if suffering from PTSD.

But in those despairingly dark and lonely days, God gave me an incredible gift. He gave me something to do with my hands and opened a portal into my heart. I had played guitar on and off my whole life, yet every attempt to write a song had failed miserably after a few embarrassingly vulnerable and petty lines.

But now, out of necessity, perhaps, I held the searing doubts and fears of my mind under the microscope of my heart, and out of the quiet space between the two, a melody flowed out of my being.

God began to teach me that He wasn't the elusive,

vengeful, predator God I had grown up believing in, waiting to pounce on me in my weakest moment. In fact, he wasn't angry at all. I was surprised to learn that, all this time, He really just wanted to talk to me. Because my relationship with Him was based on a perspective rooted in fear and timidity, I was never able to trust him.

Month by month, the fear gradually subsided and I slowly eased out of my hiding place, out into the open where I could be seen and known. And even though I wasn't quite ready to listen to what He had to say, I began to hear His soothing voice all around me. While I certainly stumbled onto this discovery because of social anxiety, I eventually learned that I really enjoyed being alone. I was able to think in ways that I could not when others were around, as I'd been too busy worrying about what they were thinking to have thoughts of my own.

The mud eventually settled to the bottom, and some semblance of balance was restored in my mind. I slowly began to believe that God wasn't waiting for the perfect opportunity to strike me down, and I suppose I became curious what He was waiting for. *Surely*, I thought, *He had no use in His Kingdom for some punk kid with social anxiety and substance issues.* I assumed He was going to have to fix me up and polish me off before I could serve the purpose He'd actually created me for, and, boy, did He have His work cut out for Him!

MY PARENTS CAME TO VISIT me several months after I'd settled into my new life in Savannah. We went out to lunch during their stay, and I remember Dad removing a letter from his pocket and handed it across the table.

"Read this," he said, "and remember it."

I proceeded to read the letter written by a woman claiming to be his daughter. Apparently, my father had a brief relationship in college (long before he'd met my mother) and had gotten the girl pregnant.

The terrified college girl made the difficult decision not to tell my dad, to simply have the baby in secret and give her up for adoption. The letter explained his daughter was living in Denver, Colorado, had four kids, and was nearing her fortieth birthday. In recent years, she'd had a growing sense that it was time to find out who her biological father was. After further investigation, she tracked him down and was surprised to find he still lived in Knoxville.

"Son, the decisions we make will follow us for the rest of our lives," Dad explained. "And now you have a sister."

Mom and Dad wrestled over the decision for a few months and eventually decided to fly out to Denver to meet his daughter and grandkids. The meeting went splendidly, and our families quickly morphed into one. I met her and the kids several months later during their visit to Knoxville and was intrigued at the thought of having a sister. I'd always wanted one, and now that I was twenty-two years old, I finally got my wish.

I SPENT THE REMAINDER OF my college years delaying the inevitability of adulthood whilst doing the bare minimum necessary to earn my degree. A renewed sense of curiosity about life began to surface, largely due to the passing of a friend and the way it impacted our community. My friend, William, was quite the thrill seeker, a kindred spirit to many in our young artist circles. His death sent shockwaves through our community and reminded us all of the fragility of life.

Conversations became more meaningful and friendships were cherished in a new and passionate way. I was strangely accustomed to death at this point. Not only had I brushed up against my own death, but I'd had several friends lose their lives in high school. The reason Will's death stood out to me was that I witnessed our community come alive and together around the tragedy of his passing, only to dissolve within a few short months. Gossip soon returned, friendships quickly decayed, and the world as we knew it became vain and petty once again. We neglected what Will's death taught us—that life is a precious gift. We forgot. We grew up.

Immediately after receiving my degree, I knew exactly what I wanted to do with the rest of my life, and I went out and did it. Not. In all sincerity, I was still terrified of the 'real world' and took my girlfriend at the time up on her offer to come live with her in Paris while she finished out her own degree in fashion design. In December 2011, I bought a one-way ticket to Paris and arrived with a classically American oversized bag . . . and a guitar. As far as I was concerned, I was living out of my true self—the mysterious, free-spirited world traveler who had convinced himself he needed very little to be very happy. As fate would have it, a wintery Paris had much to teach me about self-deception. For a city so renowned for its exquisite taste, I was shocked to find the Parisian culture in such disrepair. The people were arrogant and rude. The streets reeked of urine. Every conceivable writing surface was stained with graffiti.

As my girlfriend was preoccupied with her schooling, I spent months walking the city alone and reflecting on the fork in the road before me. For the first time in my life, the only thing I was certain of was that I knew nothing. I was keenly aware that I had no idea what I wanted from life, which was evident in my drifting. Nonetheless, I made the most of my adventure, exploring England and Spain while on that side of the pond. I wish I'd stayed longer and sat in the space of unknowing. I did what all restless travelers do when the road gets tough; for better or worse, I moved on.

AFTER MOVING BACK HOME, I bit the bullet and took a job at a friend's video production company. I decided the real world wasn't as awful as I'd imagined. You show up to work on time, pay your rent, and spend the rest of your money on food and beer. Simple enough, right? I could take care of myself, so why not bring a puppy into the mix?

Chipper was a beautiful, seven-week-old GSP I picked up from a breeder in Virginia. I brought him home to my small rental home on a farm outside town and we began living the dream. I did my best to teach him the basics, but I was hardly disciplined in my own life, and you can imagine how well this training went.

I picked up Chipper from a breeder in Virginia.

At that time, I didn't need a well-trained dog. I needed a buddy, and we were inseparable. By inseparable, I mean he basically did whatever he wanted, and I did my best to chase after him and minimize the damage. He would chew on the furniture, tear up the carpet, rip open the trash bags, and escape into the pasture behind the house to terrorize the neighbors' cattle.

It was in these almost comedic moments of helplessness that God began to reveal a fascinating dynamic in my relationship with Him.

There were times when I would take Chipper for a walk outside and, immediately upon entering the house, he would piss on the carpet. Similarly, I would buy him a chew toy and he would prefer one, or both, of my sandals. It was as if he knew what I wanted him to do, yet he would do the exact opposite. In utter frustration, I would yell at him (like that was going to make a difference), and he just sat there, looking innocent and clueless as ever.

In those moments, I felt God gently tap me on the shoulder. *"Hey, bud, sounds kinda familiar, right?"*

My jaw dropped. I couldn't deny that He was absolutely right. I was sitting there yelling at my dog for . . . being a dog, and not once did God yell at me for being . . . a human. He just gently nudged my conscience and pointed out the reflection. This happened so often, in fact, that I began to entertain the thought of one day putting all those lessons into a book. Little did I know, it was only the beginning.

I'LL NEVER FORGET ONE OF the few times I left Chipper at home while I went to work. Normally, I took him with me so he could terrorize the office, too, but that day he had to stay home. Since it was going to be an extra-long work day, I decided to let him stay out of his crate. I filled up his food and water bowls, opened the window for some fresh air, gave him a nice pat on the head, and headed to work.

Later that night, I returned home to find an empty bedroom. *Someone stole my dog,* I immediately thought (which is what every twenty-four-year-old stoner thinks when something has gone missing). I raced to the window and looked out to find a bent-up screen frame lying on the ground next to the AC unit.

Now, as the name 'Chipper' suggests, I liked the thought of my young, graceful sport pup taking a flying leap through the screen window and landing perfectly on his feet on his way to freedom. But, in all likelihood, it took every ounce of his thirty pounds of body weight to crash through the screen window. I can only imagine someone driving past the house and seeing this flailing, oblong mass of brown toppling onto the AC unit before crashing onto the ground.

Nevertheless, his prison break was a success, and the number of hours he enjoyed his freedom on the farm is, to this day, still in question.

WHILE THE PAINT WAS STILL drying on the Norman Rockwell painting I called my life, doubt seeped in and left a stain I couldn't ignore. My fear of settling down and missing out on some distant adventure was growing turbulent. Naturally, I reached for the 'eject' button.

I had always dreamt of moving to an island and living the simple life. Like most dreamers, that's about as far as I cared to look, and I figured the further along I ventured into my career, the less likely this dream would ever become a reality. I applied to a work exchange program called W.O.O.F.F. (Willing Workers On Organic Farms) and was accepted for a position on an orchid farm in Hawaii.

This was it! This was my chance to set it all aside and step into my dream world. But wait, what about Chipper? You see, the funny thing about responsibility is that you have things for which you are . . . responsible. Not to worry, I'll just find someone to look after him for a few months while I go set up our new life on an island some forty-five hundred miles away.

As fate would have it, I found someone who was up to the challenge. My boss at the time even gave his blessing to my wandering spirit and invited me to come back to work whenever my adventure concluded. This whole adventure thing was looking mighty fine from where I stood.

Two weeks into my new adventure, I got a call from Chipper's foster mom, saying he hadn't been eating and was losing a lot of weight. I figured it was separation anxiety and asked her to take him to the vet if it didn't improve in a few days.

The vet called later that week and explained separation anxiety is normal, though it rarely lasts more than a week or two. They expressed their concern and wanted to do some X-rays. I gave my consent and was happy to hear a few days later that they couldn't find anything alarming in the X-rays, though they wanted to monitor him until his condition improved.

A week or so later, the vet hospital called back and said he was getting worse. They had run some more extensive scans and found a piece of cloth wrapped around his intestines. After all the weight he had lost, they were concerned about his ability to even recover from a surgical removal. I was devastated and asked for a night to think about it, although it didn't take me long to determine that I couldn't afford a two-thousand-dollar surgery for a dog I might never see again. Regardless, they graciously offered to perform the surgery, under the condition that I signed over his custody to their hospital.

I was disappointed to hear that the terms of custody exchange required I would not even be able to inquire about his fate. I readily agreed, hoping that a miraculous surgery might enable Chipper to bless some other family in the same way he had so infinitely blessed mine. I ached for my little buddy and I still think of him often. His presence had connected me with a part of my boyhood that I didn't even know had been lying dormant in my heart.

MY ADVENTURE CONTINUED IN THE most amazing way. The orchid farm I was living on just so happened to breed Catahoula puppies. With a dozen or so dogs on the farm, there were two new litters during my time there, and my hurting heart got its fill of puppies for the rest of my stay on the big island.

More profoundly, though, was the church I encountered in the nearby town of Pahoa. For the first time in my life, the family of believers at Grassroots Church was the first community I had actively and knowingly sought. They graciously welcomed me into their thriving body, and I would never be the same.

My heart recognized a longing for community and their authenticity facilitated my first conscious and undeniable encounter with the Spirit. My friend, Elijah, invited me to join them for a night of Spirit-led worship, whatever the hell that meant. I had been enjoying a quiet night at the farm and I have to admit I was quite hesitant. Out of guilt, perhaps, I reluctantly gave in and made the drive over to their gathering. I walked in to find their worship had already begun. I quickly found a seat on the floor and did my best to settle in.

I have to back up a bit to the weeks leading up to my adventure, when a close friend had been talking to me at length about the gifts of the Spirit (not to be confused with the fruits of the Spirit). My fundamentalist upbringing knew nothing of the sort. I had never (knowingly) encountered the Spirit, much less received any of His gifts, and I was rather skeptical. Still, we prayed for these gifts, and I left for Hawaii a few days later.

Fast forward up to the worship night, as I uncomfortably sat there listening to my new friends pour out their hearts to God. I'd never heard any of the songs they were singing. As far as I could tell, there were only a few written verses to guide the melody. But the lyrics they were singing were real, unrehearsed, and wonderfully unfiltered.

My mind churned with questions—*How do they know what to say? How do they know who and when each person would sing? What in God's name am I doing here?*

I certainly didn't feel like I could engage in the singing, but sitting there listening, I was overwhelmed with a sense of desire to encounter this Spirit.

"*What do you want me to do?*" I quietly prayed.

"*Tell me what you want.*"

"*I want . . . you?*"

"*Then have me . . .* " He whispered back.

I immediately felt a warmth rise up from my soul, but the moment I recognized it, it disappeared as quickly as it had come. *Whoa, that was weird,* I thought.

As earnestly as I wanted to feel that warmth again, it did not return. The worship concluded an hour or so later, and I returned to the farm wondering what the hell had just happened.

I awoke the next morning with the same thought. I went about my morning chores. Afterward, I decided to work on a painting I had started a few days earlier.

As I sat there carefully applying each brush stroke, I

remembered my conversations with my friend back home about asking for the gifts of the Spirit. I had been especially curious about the gift of speaking in tongues. I had personally never heard someone praying in tongues, and my only knowledge of it was from the biblical account in Acts, as well as the occasional Appalachian documentary portraying snake handlers babbling on amidst their dramatic convulsions. Well, because Hawaii is an island in the middle of the Pacific Ocean, I knew there were no snakes to be handled, but I did feel a slight tug on my heart to set the paint brush down.

I pulled a pillow off the couch and sat on the living room floor. I quietly prayed, begging God to move in some clear way that I could be certain of His presence. The thought of attempting to speak in tongues was humiliating, even in an empty house. (In hindsight, this timidity was extremely indicative of a problem with the way I viewed God, but that didn't come till years later.)

"I want to speak to you, God."

"Then speak."

"No, I mean, in tongues. I want to speak to you in tongues."

Nothing.

I mustered up some syllables from God knows where, and my awkward tongue tripped over itself for a few seconds. I was embarrassed.

Nothing.

I tried again. And again. And again.

Nothing.

My heart became overwhelmed with despair. I began to weep. I wasn't even sure why I was crying, but there was apparently a lot of something that needed to come out.

The syllables began to flow. I was weeping, my mouth was overflowing and my body was on fire.

The Thrill of the Hunt

"More!" I cried. *"Please, I want more!"*

"My child, this is enough for now."

I knew He was right. I don't think I could have handled any more. This precious moment lasted for an indeterminate amount of time when I fell back to the floor in exhaustion, drenched with sweat as if I had just broken a fever.

"Thank you," I whispered as the flood of tears started to recede.

I WISH I COULD SAY after this radical encounter with the Spirit that I moved out into the jungle and started eating tree frogs, never again to speak my native tongue. But, in fact, I did just the opposite. I made plans to return home and work for the company I'd left four months prior. Turns out, clearing jungle on an orchid farm in Hawaii does wonders for the mind and body, but I knew God had other plans for my hands . . . and my tongue.

I was twenty-five when I moved back to Knoxville. I could now say that I'd done the whole island thing. Through it, I learned I wasn't quite ready to retire to the simple life. I felt like there was work to be done, and I was finally eager to do it. I wanted to use my skills and accomplish great things in the name of God's kingdom. I wanted to make music and tell stories that would inspire people to reach out toward their fullest potential. I wanted to meet a pretty girl and go out on mission and have people say how special we were, to which we would bashfully smile at each other and say, *"We're just following the Lord's plan"* or some other absurdly Christian response.

And while, on the surface, all these fantasies might sound admirable, they were, at their core, just a fancy front for my insatiable desire to be someone different than I found myself being year after year, move after move, relationship after relationship.

I didn't know what it would look like, but I knew I wanted to be better and somehow live differently. I had tried to change on so many occasions. I made vows in my despair and broke them in my rebellion. I was a mess, and I was pissed at life, myself, and God. It got to the point where I resolved to be this 'lesser' version of myself until God stepped in and did something about it. I was tired of trying, and my failures were driving me deeper into depression and addiction.

Of course, I didn't know any of this at the time and just sort of drifted through the next year or so. I did notice my family was beginning to shift into a new dynamic. My (recently discovered) sister had entered the picture a few years earlier and was becoming more of a reality in our lives. My older brother had just gotten married, and my younger brother actually moved out to live with my sister in Denver for a few months. Mom was holding down the fort while Dad was preparing to retire and sell his dental practice. We could all tell our family was entering a very different space than the one we'd just come out of. Pretty normal, right?

We were all open to this new dynamic, but we had no idea how radical of a change we were actually approaching. My sister and Dad both spent a lot of time flying back and forth from Denver. They obviously wanted to get to know each other and attempted to make up for lost time over the course of some forty years. My sister was and is still wise beyond her years, and I think Dad was able to open up to her in ways that he would not allow himself to be vulnerable with his sons, who'd always perceived him to be the model of perfection. Thankfully, she helped excavate many of his softer emotions that had lain dormant within him for twenty or more years.

I suppose the first time I ever noticed something was different about my dad happened when my mother told me she was anxious about the coming winter. He and I are both pretty seasonally affected, and his wintery depression in recent years was continuing to worsen. Mom said he'd been on medication for a while, but she didn't feel like it was helping. I didn't think that much of it, quite honestly. I was in my mid-twenties and was far too concerned with my own affairs to give much thought to his. Besides, he was superhuman, and there was no doubt in my mind that he would figure out a way to power through this and save the day like every other time.

I had always observed my dad and perceived him to be the mark of excellence. I saw his relationship with my mom, how he loved and served his family so dutifully. To this day I've never seen them argue, so I could only assume they'd somehow figured out the secret to a happy life. How effortless their lives appeared to my ultra-naïve perspective, while my life seemed to be so restless. I tried and tried and tried, but despite my best efforts, I knew my behavior was far from excellent.

What was the trick?

As we all do when we're placed in that position, I searched for something outside of me. I'd observed my mom and watched how she selflessly gave herself to the people around her. When she wasn't exhausting herself with three sons, she was volunteering at the soup kitchen or teaching a Bible study.

That must be it! I thought. *I just need to meet the right woman whose love for Jesus might inspire me to be the best version of myself, and together we can make God proud and use our gifts for His glory.*

I eventually did meet that pretty girl several months later and we dove in headfirst. The night I met her parents, she told me that her mother had given her a hug and whispered in her ear, "Is it too early to start shopping for a wedding dress?"

This kind of stuff happened all the time and we just ate it up. *We're obviously perfect for each other,* we thought, *so what are we waiting for? Let's just get married.*

About five months later, we got engaged the same week my Dad told me he was going to leave my mom. I remember him telling me, and in denial, perhaps, my thinking it would just be for a season. I figured he would move out, find whatever answer he was supposed to find, come back home and lead us to form a family band who would famously cover 'Kumbaya.'

It turns out I was gravely wrong on all accounts. Over the course of the next year and a half, my world crumbled around me.

I'd received her parents' blessing to marry her, but we quickly discovered our timeline and vision for how the wedding would go was drastically different than her mother's. Over the next several months, my fiancée and I battled with her mother over wedding details, and wounds and fears began to surface in both my relationship with my fiancée, as well as in her relationship with her mother. My fiancée and I stood by one another for a few months, but the new and increasing injuries began to take their toll.

She began to question my desire for her, and I was always quick to assure her that she was asking those questions out of her own insecurities. You see, deep down I had somehow convinced myself that God had introduced me to her so that she could save me from myself. In other words, I didn't desire her so much as I needed her to validate me. You can imagine how tumultuous a relationship that was. I expected her to be my savior, to love me despite my unbeknownst hatred of myself. But no broken human being is capable of that sort of infinite and perfect love.

Rightfully so, she was hesitant, and that just pissed me

off even more. In my state of delusion, I swallowed my pride and continued to pursue her. I honestly believed God was teaching me a lesson on desire, and if I just kept pursuing her despite her inconsistencies, she'd eventually realize that it was her insecurities and that I was the stand-up guy who stood firm in the face of chaos.

While all this was taking place, my dad continued to distance himself from the man I thought I knew. I had no idea he had been unhappy. Whenever we got together to talk, it became apparent that he had been suffering for a long time. He and Mom had been seeing a marriage counselor, but things were not looking up. He eventually told me that he wrote in his journal on my tenth birthday saying that he didn't know how much longer he wanted to stay in his marriage. He said he somehow trudged on because it was his duty, and somewhere along the way he, too, became a shadow unto himself.

He'd insisted that it was all a lie, or perhaps a half-truth at best. I told him I didn't understand. He had an amazing community of people around him, people with whom he could share anything and who had supported him through every season of life. Surely, someone would have called him out along the way. He shook his head, sobbing, and assured me it was all a lie, and it was too late. He'd been lying to himself and everyone around him for almost twenty years. He was disgusted with the disingenuous, religious pretense of the Bible Belt. He was tired of the roles he'd been playing for so long. He was deeply unhappy and felt the only way out of the trap he'd set for himself was to leave Mom or end his own life. I couldn't believe I was having this conversation with my superhuman father. It had been normal for me to share my own thoughts of suicide with him, but for him to let me into his darkness was unthinkable.

When I later shared with him how dismantling this relational shift had become and how I'd always put him on this superhuman pedestal, he responded by saying, "Being put on a pedestal is the same as being put in prison." I was astonished. I was so certain my perspective of him was accurate, but he assured me it was not. In an act of survival, his heart was crying out to be heard, but he'd lost his ability to communicate those feelings.

In a very real way, I believe God brought my sister into our lives as a way to free him from his imprisoned self. As I was quickly learning in my own life, God is more than willing to wreck his children's illusion of themselves in order to free them from their bondage.

As Dad and I began to press into these emotions we were sharing for the first time in my life, it turns out they went back far beyond twenty years. My grandfather lost both of his parents by the time he was twelve, and he practically raised himself and his younger sister through the Great Depression. He went on to fight in the Pacific Arena during World War II and again in the Korean War. He was an incredible man and provided much for his three kids, but he was never able to support them emotionally. For an orphaned twelve-year-old growing up in the Great Depression, I wondered when Grandad cut himself off from those feelings. Likely, there was no time to allow yourself to feel anything but those necessary for survival. Grandad might have never reconnected with those parts of his heart, which explains why Dad never once heard his father tell him he loved him. Dad never doubted his father's love, but he never heard it either, and there's a big difference.

My father, on the other hand, showered us with lots of love and praise, and I was curious where the reverse happened. He said it was emotionally devastating to never hear your father say a simple "I love you, son," and Dad vowed to never let an opportunity go by to not convey those feelings to his own boys. He would show up at every swim meet, pick us up from school every chance he got, and be there for us a thousand other ways to remove any doubt that he loved us and was there for us in every way imaginable. But somewhere in the midst of all that loving sacrifice, some part of his own identity was being neglected. Again, I was so consumed by his love, nor did I have the emotional wherewithal, to stop and think about his heart and the feelings associated with it.

Growing up, I'd only seen his lighter emotions. Laughter, joy, pride when we'd done something well, even his disappointment and frustration were conveyed with an abiding gentleness. But now, for the first time, I was seeing fear, doubt, shame, deep anger, and despair. These weren't the emotions of a superhuman. These darker feelings, they sounded like those of a little boy crying out for love. They sounded like me.

Amidst all the sadness and despair that came with my parents' divorce, I was grateful that I now had a much fuller understanding of who my father was. Even though we were both still deeply wounded, our hearts finally occupied a place of authenticity. What had transpired released him from the prison cell pedestal I'd confined him to; in turn, it released me from an unrealistic mark of excellence that I was subconsciously pursuing as a way to validate my purpose and earn God's love. It also gave me permission to feel all the emotions of my heart without shame or fear of it challenging my manhood.

MY FIANCÉE AND I EVENTUALLY grew so exhausted of fighting with her mother that we called off the engagement and went back to dating. Things almost instantly cleared back up. It was still a bit awkward at family gatherings, but we wrote off the feelings as water under the bridge and repressed them for later, of course.

We dated for another six months, and I worked up the courage to ask her to marry me again. After all, I was certain she was a gift from God, and in my mind, I was mastering this idea of pursuit. I assured her that I'd meant what I said about spending my life with her, and she assured me that she would not take off the ring again.

We announced that the engagement was back on, though I could never convince her to pick a date. I told her I'd wait as long as she needed, but that I'd prefer to have a date that we were working toward as a team. For whatever reason, she could not bring herself to do so. She bought a wedding dress, even purchased my wedding ring, but no wedding plans were being made.

This, of course, raised concerns with all parties involved. As we pressed into her hesitation, it became apparent that I was not living up to the person she needed me to be in order to feel good about marrying me. Despite my best efforts, I was unable to meet her expectations.

For me, as someone who was unaware and yet deeply motivated by shame, this revelation perpetuated my self-hatred and reinforced my suspicions that I was unlovable.

How ridiculous those attempts were and how impossible a task it is to be someone you're not! This betrayal of the self only deepens one's self-hatred, and that's exactly what happened as we continued to pursue an illusion of one another. We came away from our true selves and ultimately began to resent one another for carving out the shell of a person we now inhabited.

I wondered where God was in the midst of all my pain

and confusion. Why was He not coming to my rescue? Why was He letting me torment myself with depression and heartache year after year? Did He not care that I was trying to be better?

The straw that broke the camel's back came on my birthday, of all days. I often smile when I recall the irony of that fateful day for our relationship. Knoxville is one of those cities that completely shuts down at the first sign of snow, all except the bars, of course. To my delight, I was gifted with an incredible snow day on my twenty-eighth birthday, and it still stands as my best birthday to date. Work was cancelled and we had all day to prepare for one of my favorite bluegrass bands that was to play later that evening at the historic Bijou Theatre. We spent the day frolicking in the snowy streets of downtown Knoxville. I was beside myself the entire day, simply because I'd forgotten my heart could feel so full. I wondered if things were beginning to finally turn in our favor, and I was excited at even the slightest possibility that we were stepping into the future we'd been longing for.

Before the show, twenty of my closest friends amassed at the restaurant beside the theatre, where we ate and drank to our hearts' content. This poses a potential problem for someone with an almost insatiable appetite for alcohol. I've never been someone who goes overboard when indulging out of sadness. Every time I've gotten myself in trouble by having too much to drink has been during a celebration (i.e. the best day I'd had in two years). A normal person might have a few drinks and sit back to enjoy the rest of the evening. You should know by now that I'm far from normal.

Up to this point, the night was still going great, but that was about to change. A friend had gifted me with a really nice bottle of scotch for my birthday, and, in the middle of the show, he offered to go out to the car and fill up his flask so we could enjoy it during the performance. I handed him the car keys and completely forgot about it till he showed up minutes later with the flask in hand. We both took a generous sip and returned our attention to the incredible evening.

An hour or so later, my fiancée said she was ready to go home. I was, of course, in no condition to drive, so I reached in my pocket to give her the keys. Guess what? There were no keys in my pocket, and my boozed-up brain could not recall that I'd given them to my friend during the show. Not surprisingly, she was less than enthused that I'd lost the keys to her car. She was, however, very enthusiastic about letting me know she was unhappy. We bickered in the lobby for a while before she ordered us an Uber back to my house, where she would happily drop me off to sober up . . . alone.

I woke up the next morning knowing I was in trouble. I didn't know how much in trouble I was until I got over to her place and attempted to smooth things out. I repeated empty promises, but it was too late. It was over. I pleaded with her to reconsider, just one more chance to prove I could be better, but she stood her ground.

She understandably did not want to stand around while I moved my belongings out of her house. And as she got in her car to drive away, she told me something I'll never forget.

"You have to lose it all, Rob. You're never going to change until you hit rock bottom, and I can't go there with you."

Who could blame her? I certainly didn't. I spent the next few hours packing my belongings into a trailer I borrowed from work. We weren't living together at the time, but the house she was renting was going to be the house we lived in together once we got married. That being the case, I had about 80 percent of the belongings I didn't use on a daily basis housed over at her place instead of renting out a storage unit.

The Thrill of the Hunt

She was moving on, which meant I was moving out. I was sad, angry, and everything in between. I repeated empty vows to God to truly live differently from then on, you know, all the normal things people say when they think they've lost everything but really have no idea.

After I packed the trailer, I decided I'd had enough moving for one emotionally charged weekend and determined to park the trailer at my apartment for a few days instead of immediately moving my stuff into a storage unit. Two days later, the entire trailer was stolen out in front of my apartment. I laughed about it then, and I laugh about it now. After everything that had happened, it was all too perfect to sum up my twenty-eighth birthday. She was right—I did have to lose everything, although I don't think this was exactly what she was talking about. No, that would come months later, when my 'F*** it' mentality would land me at a very rocky bottom.

While my broken engagement and parents' divorce were two of the most painfully traumatic experiences of my life, it began the process of liberating me from my own performance-based mentality. When my dad broke out of the superhuman mold I'd confined him to, so too did the illusion that I had to live up to this superhuman standard in order to be lovable.

It was a monumental shift in my life as God began to show me that I have my own path to walk, and it will never look like my dad's or anyone else's. I was free to discover who He made me to be instead of trying to fit into some mold of who I thought I was supposed to be. I still hold my dad in the highest regard, but he doesn't have to be perfect anymore, and neither do I.

Nonetheless, I still believe God smiles on the way a son looks up to his father. The way a son tries to live in a way that would make his father proud, even though, and I'm speaking of a good father here, the son could not possibly do anything to make his father less proud of him. A good father beams in the presence of his offspring. It's a reflection of the way God delights in his children adoring him.

THIS TRANSFORMATION, OF COURSE, TOOK place over several months. At the time, all I knew was that I felt lost. The shattered illusions of who I was supposed to be piled up around my feet, and I often wondered if I was losing my mind.

The unanswerable questions led me to hate myself even more. I felt like everyone around me knew who they were and what they were supposed to be doing with their lives. I, on the other hand, could not stop feeling like an epic failure. And without a reference for who I was supposed to be, I subconsciously developed a reckless mentality that eventually led to my accident. I wasn't exactly trying to hurt myself, but the concept of caution was laughable.

I wondered if I'd one day be one of those people on the street just screaming incoherent thoughts at invisible people. It didn't seem that far-fetched. No one else was talking about the fears and doubts I was clearly experiencing, so I could only assume I was on the frontier of sanity. My heart raced with these spiraling thoughts. What could possibly be worse than going insane—than losing your grip on reality?

I'd heard a sermon several years earlier that juxtaposed demon possession and insanity. I don't entirely remember the context of the sermon; I only remember the pastor referencing the Latin word *sanus*, which translates to *clean*. Therefore, *insanus* would translate to *unclean*.

I'd never really thought of insanity in terms of uncleanliness. When I think of insanity, I usually think of straitjackets, padded rooms, and Russell Crowe (only because of his role in *A Beautiful Mind*. Sorry, Russell). Without this translation, I would never have made the connection between unclean and insanity.

But if we use the word *insane* in this spiritual context, anyone who is stained by sin is definitively insane. Years later when I recalled the word, this was especially comforting to someone like myself who, at the time, was genuinely concerned with losing my mind. I wondered if it was possible that we are all just stumbling around in the dark, chasing after our own gratification and never having enough. Einstein defined insanity as doing the same thing over and over expecting a different result, and surely this sort of perpetual dissatisfaction would be insane, right?

In biblical times, when leprosy was prevalent, the Jewish people had a law that required anyone with leprosy to walk through the streets screaming, *"Unclean! Unclean!"* This was to allow bystanders plenty of time to clear out of the way so they wouldn't come in contact with the diseased.

As such, lepers were all but entirely cast out of society. It was generally believed that leprosy was God's punishment for a certain sin—their lot in life—so while the natural outcasting served the purpose of quarantining the diseased, it was also a cultural representation of the way sin separates people from God. The law also insisted that lepers tear their clothing to further symbolize their despair.

Is God punishing me? I wondered. *There must be some explanation for why my life is being turned on its head.*

In my own bouts of insanity, I'd recall this phrase—*"Insanus! Insanus!"*—and couldn't help but relate. It seemed like every other week somebody was getting married, buying a house, or announcing another child was on the way. Don't get me wrong; I was genuinely happy for my friends and family. I just felt deeply shameful to watch them progress through life so seemingly effortlessly while mine was spiraling out of control and I was doing everything I could to survive a crash landing.

To some of you that might seem melodramatic, but I can assure you anyone who's ever battled with harsh rejection, endless depression, helpless addiction, sudden illness, or heinous sexual assault could relate to these feelings of losing their mind.

"Unclean! Unclean! Give way, lest you, too, be cursed!"

With my face covered in shame, I'd take each step as the seemingly sane around me gasped and gave a wide berth. I wanted to clothe every inch of my skin so that no one could see the severity of my condition. But through my tattered clothes, I knew they could see the reality of my disease rotting away my flesh, and one could hardly be blamed for wanting to keep their distance.

You must understand that this is a common truth for humanity. Whatever perception we have of ourselves is what we project out into the world. In my case, I viewed myself as diseased and, therefore, unlovable. Subconsciously, I pushed people away whenever they got close. Because of their own fears and insecurities, a quite normal response to being pushed away is to simply walk away.

It would take someone pretty radical to approach a person with that sort of incurable disease and somehow convince them their true worth is still wholly intact, right? But as the crowd cleared the way while I walked through life, there stood the Messiah holding his ground. I'd surely heard of Him, but I didn't recognize Him. I always thought I would, but I didn't. He'd been standing there my entire life telling me who He was, but I couldn't believe Him. I wouldn't. No one could be that loving to such a wretched, unlovable creature.

"Unclean. Unclean." I insisted, trying to step around

Him. But He cut me off with a smile. *"Unclean. Unclean."* I sobbed as He opened his arms to embrace me.

"Who told you that?" He asked. *"Rob, you're my son. You keep trying to fix the hole in your heart. You've even asked me to fix it. But I don't want to fix it. I want to fill it. I know all you can see is your brokenness, but come talk to me and let me tell you what I see."*

My lifelong wrestling with His love had taken me to the mat, and I was exhausted. That's when He pinned me down, and instead of telling me how stupid and disappointing I had been, He whispered His eternal love into my exhausted heart. For the first time, I couldn't squirm out of this one. I eagerly tapped out. Again, to my surprise, Jesus helped me to my feet and lifted my arm in triumph.

"Clean! Clean! Love is victorious and I declare this man clean!"

When I thought I'd lost it all, and indeed I had, I encountered a Jesus who had been waiting for me my entire life. He wasn't angry or impatient. In fact, He was exuberant and eager to help me see that all the things I was searching for in my external circumstances and relationships could only be realized in His personhood. He showed me how no human being is able to quench the longing in my heart, nor could I ever modify my behavior enough to justify myself before God to earn His Love.

Upon meeting Jesus, I no longer needed a wife to show me the love and validation for which I was yearning. I no longer needed to act a certain way so that I could make strides toward becoming the superhuman I thought my father was. This was my first taste of true freedom, and it came from losing it all.

My darkest fears came true as Jesus removed the religious blockades that obstructed His love from entering my heart. One by one, He plucked them away until all I could see was His smiling face, and all I could hear was His resounding love for me. With nothing standing in the way, I could stand before Him unashamed. I was finally beginning to believe that He is who He says He is, and I am who He says I am. He's a good, good Father, and I am His beloved son. Period. End of discussion.

IN THE MOST MIRACULOUS WAY, God used all these traumatic events to show me how He felt about me specifically. God doesn't throw a soft blanket of love over all of His children and generalize His affections for them. God singled me out and declared His immense joy in being my Father, my Good Master who provides for me and pursues me to no end.

The revelation in the pasture didn't answer all the questions my mind has toiled with over the years; it did, however, offer something much more fulfilling. Much like Chip's electric fence, it established a boundary within which I can safely observe the present life all around me. While the space itself is timeless, I often catch myself venturing too closely to the perimeter, either to glance back to the shame of my past or warily eye the fears of my future. I'm tempted to step out of safety and return to my old way of thinking and seeing, where I tried to manipulate circumstances in order to achieve some elusive, optimized version of myself.

I liken this space to the balcony I jumped from three years ago now. The view of the lake and the Cherokee Mountain wilderness encircling it is majestic and *could* have been more than enough to scratch whatever adventurous itch I attempted to appease through the stunt. Instead of being grateful for the landscape before me and the peace all around me, I insisted on needing more. More life. More thrill. More . . . pain.

But in those moments when I look out from the safety around me and wonder what adventures lie beyond the threshold, I remember the chains and anguish of bondage. I remember that I've been given new eyes to see. I'm learning to be content within this space and let those regrets and fears pass by, knowing the answers (if I need them at all) will come in due time.

As I walk through life, slowly giving up my obsessive need to have control, Jesus often uncovers parts of my heart where He is presently not enough, or rather, where I doubt His promise to be enough for me there. The Jesus I encounter in those moments is far more real than any Jesus I hoped to make proud by falsely 'taking up my cross' and trudging on through life wounded, bitter, and guarded. Since I no longer need to earn His love and acceptance, it frees me up to be honest when we come across one of these wounds. When I confess that I don't yet trust Him to fulfill me there, He doesn't get upset; He doesn't leave me to figure it out by myself. He simply sits with me in that space, and I can ask Him to show me the parts of my past that are now keeping me from being able to trust in His fullness.

You see, venturing into the past on my own is dangerous because it's limited to my perspective and the emotions that drove my actions. But when I walk in stride with Jesus and hear His perspective of what transpired, where He was in the midst of all my striving, the wounds begin to heal and a burden of shame is lifted from my heart.

IT'S NEARLY IMPOSSIBLE FOR SOMEONE with a limp to hide it very well. To anyone who's paying attention whatsoever, it's puzzlingly noticeable, even if they don't voice their concern. People often ask, "I noticed you're limping. Everything OK?"

I smile and say something like, "You bet your sweet ass I'm OK. I can walk!" or "Yeah, but you should see the other guy."

That's usually about the time they cock an eyebrow and walk away wondering what the hell I've been smoking. Every once in a while, someone will go so far as to ask what happened, and I get to tell them all about the time I decided to be my own stunt double and I lost my role as the lead actor in what I thought was my own movie.

Sometimes they get it; others smirk and say, "I bet you don't do something stupid like that again."

Hmm, I think, *that's doubtful.*

This assumption raises a series of interesting questions, though. How often do we live in such ways as to avoid the inevitability of our humanity? If wounds are a reality of life, then pain is merely a byproduct of that reality. Are we to hide from the possibility of pain? Should we throw a cloak over our wounds and insist there's nothing to be seen? Should I minimize my steps so that no one can see my limp?

I think not, nor is it likely that I'll ever succeed in being anything other than myself. When I broke my back, I was answering the call of my inner longing for adventure. While many might see it as a fatal flaw, I truly love that part of myself. Enveloped within the one story I tell of how I came to walk with a slight limp, there's a thousand other times that I missed all that Life was offering. Now that is something stupid you can bet I won't do again, at least on purpose, anyway.

With Jesus now teaching me how to walk, I've begun to revel in the scars we humans bear. Make no mistake, our scars are not punishment for our sinfulness. Jesus alone bears the scars of that punishment. Ours are merely the consequences of our actions, of living in the frailty of fallen humanity. Each of them has a curious story of how it came to be, and even more fascinating is the body's natural desire to heal itself.

Could it be that our wellness is greater than our disease, or that our wholeness is more telling than our fractional selves? What if our lives are infinitely more blessed than they could ever be cursed, and if so, how could that knowledge transform us?

EXPLORING THE BOUNDARIES OF MY new freedom, I've begun the process of accepting myself with limps, scars, warts and all. To my amazement, when the presence of Jesus instills the awareness of my boundaries, the boundaries of my awareness are heightened, deepened, and broadened. As Jesus invites me to love even the ugliest parts of myself, I'm now free to love even the ugliest parts of the people around me. I don't always do so, but the awareness itself gives me a choice in the matter, and I no longer have to suffer under the burden of another person's shortcomings. If I allow another person's actions to bother me, that is by my own choosing and not theirs.

Furthermore, my unwillingness to love a certain 'flaw' in someone else is a direct indication that I still have a festering wound that needs to be touched by Jesus. It's important to ask myself, *What about this person's behavior is causing me such irritation?* and keep an eye toward the areas of our own behavior that we probably haven't learned to love yet. Unless we learn to accept these 'flaws' about ourselves, it's impossible for us to allow even Jesus to love them. But these wounds we bear are not only inevitable; they're vital. They are the very portals of grace by which Jesus redeems the lost parts of His children. He shines His Light on the wounds, that each of them may be seen, found, and declared to be beautiful and fully lovable.

After Jesus's death abolished the laws of the Old Testament, His resurrection declared a new command to those who claim to follow Him:

"Love one another. As I have loved you, so you must love one another. By this everyone will know that you are my disciples, if you love one another." (John 13:34-35)

When we know the reality of Jesus's love despite our multitude of transgressions, He invites us to follow Him along the most daring adventure imaginable. He gives us new eyes to see people as He sees them and a heart to love them as He loves them. In doing so, He places within us a longing for everyone we encounter to share in that freedom.

But that can be a scary thought—to truly love another as boldly as Jesus loves us. That could get awkward real fast, huh? How are we supposed to explain the magnitude of what's taken place in our hearts? What if they find out about our past and accuse us of hypocrisy? What if we can't save them, and we once again let Jesus down?

These were the questions that plagued me for years, and these were the lies that I unknowingly hid behind for fear that if brought out into the open, the world would see that I was naked, ashamed, and alone.

But in the eternal seconds after my ungracious fall from 'glory,' all those lies came crashing down around me. Indeed, I was naked, meaning I could not hide what had just happened. I was ashamed and exhausted after years of trying to cover my nakedness. I was alone in that I found myself dashed about the rocks under my own compulsion. Yet lying there, I felt strangely known.

All my deepest fears had just become a reality. Looking up, all I had was my sight, and as far as I'm concerned, I was seeing for the first time. I once heard it said that Jesus isn't so much interested in changing the circumstances in our lives as He is in changing the way we see them.

This insight could not be more inverted from the conventional Christian perspective. So often in the turmoil and strife of life, we beg Jesus to change the circumstances of our lives. We don't care how He does is, we just want it done, and we want it done immediately. How worldly of us to ask God to take away the very pain that is pointing directly to wounds in our hearts that sincerely need a touch from Jesus. And yet we do; we just want the pain and discomfort gone so we can go on living with hearts half-alive.

You think Jesus ever had tension in His life? Remember, there was only a very brief period of His ministry where the entirety of the conventional church at the time didn't want Him dead. I'm sure it wasn't easy corralling His disciples (many of them teenagers at the time) and preparing them to pick up where He left off. Yet there was a stillness about Him. He was fully submitted to the will of His Father and completely disregarded His own interests or comfort. Jesus found fulfillment in doing the work His Father set before Him. He did not allow His view of God's children to be perverted by the curse of sin. In being fully alive and present to the people around Him, He embodied the glory of God.

This is what it looks like to follow Jesus, whose unconditional acceptance empowers us to merely sit in the discomfort and tension of daily life. We don't need to hide our wounds. We don't need to cover our fears and pretend they're not there. We don't have to clean up our act before we can kneel at the foot of the cross and worship the one who stood in our place. That's not the point of coming to the altar. The point of coming to the altar is to have an encounter with Jesus. That can't happen if we're not willing to be honest with ourselves, with each other, and most importantly, with Jesus.

In this place of honest vulnerability, we can talk to Jesus about our discomfort. We ask Him to reveal the hidden wounds in our hearts that deeply need His loving touch. Sometimes He blesses us with revelation. Other times, He invites us to simply find rest at His side, and that, my friends, is a revelation unto itself. In those moments of clarity, Life illuminates life, and we view our long journey with a sense of gentle excitement. We look back, if only to see how far we've come, and realize that Jesus has been with us since the very beginning. We did not always have eyes to see Him, but He was there in the crowd, and He is here now. At any moment, we have the freedom to approach the Master and enter into his joy.

Yonah guarding the shoreline from a gaggle of geese.

This was my first attempt to teach Yonah about the importance of contrast in photography.

8

Oh, How Far We've Come

"The gospel is this: We are more sinful and flawed in ourselves than we ever dared believe, yet at the very same time we are more loved and accepted in Jesus Christ than we ever dared hope."[1]

— Tim Keller, *The Meaning of Marriage*

"A song of ascents. Of David. My heart is not proud, Lord, my eyes are not haughty; I do not concern myself with things too great and too marvelous for me. But I have calmed and quieted myself. I am like a weaned child with his mother. Like a weaned child I am content."

— Psalm 131: 1-2

It's HARD TO BELIEVE I'VE HAD YONAH FOR ONLY A FEW SHORT YEARS. There's not a half an hour that passes by without me thinking about him, and I'm confident he'd say the same if you spoke his language. This bond we've developed is truly one of the most beautiful mysteries I've ever gotten to explore. Two lowly creatures with a simple, unspoken agreement—no matter where we are or what we're doing, it's going to be an adventure.

Recall how he threw up all over my trunk only a mile or two down the road after I picked him up from the breeder. When we got on the interstate to head back to Tennessee, he just sat there looking out the rear window at the bright blue world passing by. Until that morning, he had no idea how big the world was or that I even existed. All of a sudden, we were traveling through it together. We were strangers back then, but, boy, did we have a fun future ahead of us.

It wasn't so long ago that I had to coax Yonah into the car every time I wanted to take him somewhere. Even then he had to ride in the crate just so he wouldn't drool all over my newly leased vehicle. Now, he's as happy to jump in the car as he is to run straight into the woods.

The truth is—Yonah doesn't care where we're going. Either way, we're in for an adventure. He's so willing and excited; it's easy to forget he wasn't always like this. Somewhere along the way, he began to see the car as a magic portal connecting home with some grand, far-off exploration just waiting to be had. In fact, the car ride has become just another part of the adventure and he happily sticks his head out the window to let his ears flap in the wind. (I find it especially entertaining when he sits in the passenger seat and leans into the turns, and I'm convinced he'd make a wonderful driver had he been bestowed the gift of thumbs.)

It's funny; now that he's transitioning into adolescence, he's showing signs of maturity. He's still a puppy through and through, but I've noticed a shift. Shortly after his second birthday, we had just laid down in my bedroom, when we both heard the leaves crunching outside the window. He perked up and began to growl. I wasn't too worried. It could have been any number of animals lacking opposable thumbs, and I was fairly certain whatever it was could not open the basement door. Nonetheless, I couldn't help but smile as Yonah sat at attention for half an hour till he was convinced I was safe from whatever danger had made the noise.

For you dog owners with more protective breeds, that probably doesn't sound so heroic. While he's never been territorial, I couldn't help but smile at the sign that he's coming into his own. He's my animal. I'm his person. I didn't bring him into my home so that I could clean dog crap off the carpet for a couple months, nor did I invite him into my life so that I could cater to his every need. I didn't train him because I needed to feel dominant over another creature. No, I did all these things so that he would become the perfect companion. I bear his frustrating transgressions, and he deals with mine. That's simply what you do for your companions in order to explore the fullness of life together.

When two beings have a deep bond with one another, their hearts are aligned. They find joy in the same things. They delight in each other's presence. There's authenticity about their relationship that is clearly evident to anyone observing. A bond so real, in fact, that someone observing might even find themselves slightly jealous of that sort of connection. I certainly know I do. When I see an elderly couple who are deeply in love, more in love than when they were first married, I envy it. I witness something that they have and I don't, and in the space between those two places, I recognize my desire for it.

In those moments of observing that sort of bond, it's easy to forget about the struggles that forged that connection. When I read about the great champions of faith in the Bible, I do the same thing. I mentioned earlier about the wisdom of King Solomon, how I naively imagined him to wake up one morning after asking God for wisdom, and he suddenly was the wisest man that ever lived. In a moment we'll talk about Elijah, who asked God to withhold rain from the Kingdom of Israel, and God did so for three and a half years. From my perspective, that's a pretty powerful bond.

There is someone in the Bible, though, who might not be so quick to forget about the hard times that befell him and the crisis of faith that often resulted. We opened our conversation with a psalm from King David. Talk about a basket case. That guy was all over the place! In between the most beautifully poetic thoughts and songs ever written to God, David was on the verge of a mental meltdown. Even within the same psalms, David often seems to ride an emotional rollercoaster that still throws me for a loop.

It is funny, though, to recall many times in my teenage years when I'd open my Bible hoping for a word of inspiration and, after choosing a psalm at random, landed on one of his many bouts of despair. Let's just say I didn't always walk away with the confidence I'd hoped might slay the day's Goliath.

But there he was—King David, a man after God's own heart—who, for the record, is the only man in the scriptures to be dubbed that title. How could this be? What was the difference between King David and the dozens of other legendary fathers of faith written about in the Bible?

Well, amidst his many victories and equally infamous moments of weakness, one thing that is acutely noticeable is David's honesty. He wasn't afraid to tell God how he felt. He didn't hold back when he wanted to give God the proverbial finger (not sure if that was invented at the time, but you get the gist).

David was honest, even when life wasn't going the way he hoped, and at the end of the majority of his anguishing rants, we recognize a stillness that washes over him. Somewhere amidst the dramatic peaks and valleys of his emotions, a deep peace resided in David's heart.

There is a childlikeness about King David that God adored so evidently. I wonder where that comes from?

In addition to David's courage and honesty that I so righteously envy, I admire his submission. Some of my favorite psalms feature David's wonder at the mystery of

God. In the same breath of offering God praise, David surrendered his own need for understanding.

"Such infinite thoughts are too wonderful for me. It is too high; I cannot reach it," he proclaims in Psalm 139:6.

David delighted in the meditations of his heart, claiming moments later that his attempt to number them would be impossible. What I love about this so much is that he continued to meditate on them nonetheless. Even though he couldn't understand them and didn't insist upon doing so, he honestly found deep joy in simply pondering God's ways.

Even more beautiful is that God, too, delights in the meditations of our hearts. God loves to be sought after, even though we could never fully comprehend Him. Perhaps the greatest transformation in my life has come from God revealing His delight in me. This is the thrill of the hunt—to seek and to find, to be sought and to be found.

Before encountering the true God, the God I believed in was perpetually disappointed with me. I'd read the stories about God being pleased with those who follow Him, but from my perspective at that time, following Him meant never messing up. Therefore, I understood God to be angry, disappointed, frustrated, tiresome, ready for me to grow up. But I viewed Him through the lens of shame and was, therefore, unable to see the emotions that more closely resemble His true nature.

Throughout the Bible, God displays a vast range of emotions, and I often forget our emotions were made in God's likeness, not the other way around. There are several mentions in the Bible of God growing tired of Israel's rebellion. I struggled for so long trying to comprehend how God can claim to be jealous, angry, vengeful and exhausted, yet still claim that I could never be separated from His love.

Surely, this timeless God I'd heard about is the same God in the Old Testament as in the New.

If this is the same God that claims to never leave me, I thought, then why the hell don't I feel His presence? Why can't I see Him do anything that would evoke some change in my life so I can be free from these chains that remind me of every failure I've ever done?

It was through those thoughts and moments that a dear friend and brother pointed out where I was directing my questions. I was in awe. I had been voicing my complaints and frustrations to myself and anyone else who would listen, but I never aimed them at God. My friend encouraged me to address God with those concerns.

"He's a big God," my friend reminded me. "He can handle it."

I figured it couldn't hurt, and the next quiet moment I found, I unleashed the full fury of Robert Daniel Crawford. I know—terrifying, right? But to my surprise, after I came to the end of my exhausted rant, I felt a certain sense of peace, as if He'd actually heard me.

I cried, screamed, and cursed every frustration that came to mind, and once I got it all out, I felt God smiling upon me.

I didn't have the awareness at the time, but that was probably the first real conversation I'd ever had with God. As I recall, I felt like He was proud of me, excited even, at what I'd said. My incoherent rant of expletives with a couple of valid frustrations peppered in was enough to somehow make the God of the universe smile. It was honest . . . and it felt so good.

"God, if I'd have known that's all it took to make you smile, I'd have tried that years ago," I said, now speaking directly to Him, rather than about Him, hoping He might hear

me. After I told God how I felt about Him from a heart of honesty rather than a mind of impersonal knowledge, we had a new dialogue that allowed me to hear how He felt about me.

In the following years, I would experience a vast number of peaks and valleys reminiscent of King David's life, and my heart was eventually led to a place where I, too, could proclaim, *"I will give thanks and praise to You, for I am fearfully and wonderfully made. Wonderful are your works, and my soul knows it right well."*

How do you feel about that thought? Are you in awe of who God has made you to be? If you're like me, it's next to impossible to believe how deeply loved and well-thought-out we are. Especially when our lives seem so chaotic, we have a hard time seeing that God is with us and that He is delivering us from the hands of our enemy—those parts of ourselves that are enslaved and hiding in shame from the One who made us.

Maybe we should rethink our definition of a satisfied soul. If our only understanding of satisfaction is a deep sense of contentment, peace and joy, what happens when frustration and tension inevitably enter the picture? Again, if God experiences the full spectrum of emotions, not all of them tied up in a pretty bow, does that mean He is not satisfied with Himself?

I think we'd all do well to let go of our tiny perspectives and ask God to open our eyes and hearts to His definition of a full life. That means letting go of outcomes and attachments, even to our perspective of right and wrong, in order to simply experience the life in and all around us.

God's love is fierce, reckless, and if you're experiencing the discomfort of your present circumstances, I encourage you to direct your frustrations to the God before you instead of the world around you. What is it about His invitation to honesty that's so painful? Are you afraid of being exposed?

I've got news for you, my friend. God made you, and He sees you, and He knows you. If you're afraid of being honest, as I was for so many years, you're missing out on the wonderful things He wants to tell you about yourself. He'll knock you on your ass with all the unimaginable beauty He's packed into your now frightened heart. And I hate to tell you (not really) there's a type of comfort and joy that the Lord wants to give you that can only be experienced in the darkness of the wilderness and the waste places.

Of course, if you're not ready for that level of honesty, that's fine, too. He's not going anywhere, and He's got all the time in the world.

I'M GOING TO GO OUT on a limb here and assume we're all familiar with the story of Elijah and how he challenged 450 prophets of the false god Baal. If you haven't heard it, I implore you to check it out in 1 Kings 18. It's one of the most epic displays of faith *ever*, and perhaps we'd all do well to revisit the story. Anyway, after Elijah pissed off the entirety of the powers-that-were back in the day (by that, I mean 900 B.C.), he feared for his life and went into hiding.

Which begs the question, *"Why, dude?"*

I mean, God had just rained down a fireball from heaven that not only incinerated the sacrificial bull it was intended for but also the stones that made up the altar, not to mention the water-filled trench surrounding it. As if that weren't enough, God went on to end a three-and-a-half-year drought that threatened to wipe out the entire nation of Israel, all because Elijah asked God to do so.

That took some pretty serious faith, so why did Elijah now feel the need to escape the wrath of Ahab and Jezebel, the measly king and queen of Israel? One would imagine, after such a public manifestation of the glory of God, that his faith would cause him to stand firm against any worldly consequences that might have befallen his ministry.

Regardless of his intentions, Elijah fled, and somewhere along the journey he grew so weary and distraught that he asked God to take his life.

He essentially said in his misery, *"God, this is some B.S. and I'm over it. Just kill me. I'm no different than everybody else. Why should I suffer this burden if all of my efforts make no difference to the people you've sent me to help?"*

In Matthew Henry's thorough commentary of the incident (from which I'm greatly borrowing this insight), Henry suggests that God left Elijah to himself. After all, Elijah had willfully fled from the task God sent him to endure, and perhaps God was showing him that his moment of courage and strength before the prophets of Baal was made possible by God's might alone. In truth, Elijah was, by himself, no better than the people around him.

For both Elijah's sake and ours, God did not answer the prayer to end his life. Instead, God let him fall asleep in his misery under a broom tree. After however many hours of rest, an angel of the Lord roused him from his sleep. Elijah woke and was surprised to find a jar of water and a loaf of bread baking on a bed of hot stones right there next to him. Elijah had his fill of the bread and water . . . and fell asleep again. This dude was tired, and we need not wonder why. The angel later woke him a second time and said, *"Get up, man. Eat some more food. You have a long road ahead of you."*

Elijah obeyed and was strengthened by the Lord's provision that, by the way, appeared out of seemingly nowhere. He proceeded forty days and forty nights to Mount Horeb, the

same mountain where God delivered the Ten Command-
ments to Moses (cough, cough . . . twice).

When Elijah got to the mountain, he took shelter in a
cave and probably took a nap. That's about the time he heard
God say something along the lines of, *"Elijah, why are you
hiding?"*

Elijah replied, *"C'mon, God. You saw what just happened. You did what just happened, and I did what you asked
me to do in front of all your people. Now they're trying to kill
me. What else do you want me to do?"*

God replied, *"Come out of the cave and stand before me."*

**"And behold, the Lord passed by, and a great and strong
wind tore the mountains and broke in pieces the rocks before
the Lord, but the Lord was not in the wind. And after the
wind, an earthquake, but the Lord was not in the earthquake. And after the earthquake, a fire, but the Lord was not
in the fire. And after the fire, the sound of a low whisper. And
when Elijah heard it, he wrapped his face in his cloak and
went out and stood at the entrance of the cave. And behold,
there came a voice to him and said, 'What are you doing
here, Elijah?'"**

—1 Kings 19:11-13

Again, Elijah pleaded his case by making excuses.

And in a gentleness reserved only for the Lord God Almighty, Yahweh replied, *"Go back to the place I sent you.
You're right in saying that my people have not listened to my
words, but a few of them actually do have ears. Follow my instructions, and I will spare them."* (Paraphrasing 1 Kings
19:15-18)

I DON'T THINK IT'S A stretch to draw parallels between Elijah's
life and so many others, including my own, who've gone into

hiding for various reasons. Granted, I never summoned down fireballs from heaven, so I suppose we'll have to cross that one off the list. But I do find it comforting to know that a man of such great faith also experienced a tremendous amount of doubt, frustration, and exhaustion.

How often do we resolve that we've come to our end? We cannot go any further, and in our wearied plight, we lie down to wallow in self-pity. From our micro-perspective of the happenings of our lives, we can see no path, no lighthouse to direct our course through the stormy night. Paradoxically, we falsely surrender our will out of spite and are driven into a deeper wilderness, determined upon an encounter with the God.

Sure enough, Elijah was roused from his slumber to find himself not only provided for by an angel of the Lord, but also that he had been guarded throughout the night. His strength was replenished by this realization, but the Bible says nothing about his faith being renewed as he pressed on for forty days and forty nights until he reached his destination. God didn't call him to Mount Horeb; that was Elijah's own choosing. He didn't even know why he was going to the mountain, only that he must go, as if he was fully expectant for God to meet him there.

Matthew Henry notes, "God knows what He designs us for, though we do not, what service, what trials, and will take care for us when we, for want of foresight, cannot for ourselves, that we be furnished for them with grace sufficient. He that appoints what the voyage shall be will victual the ship accordingly. . . . God will take care of his outcasts; and those who, for his sake, are driven out from among men, he will find, and own, and gather with everlasting loving-kindnesses. . . . It concerns us often to enquire whether we be in our place and in the way of our duty. 'Am I where I should be, whither God calls me, where my business lies, and where I may be useful?'"[2]

After Elijah came to the cave, (a metaphor, perhaps, for the depths of our hiding), God answered him for the first time since he asked God to reveal himself before the prophets of Baal and the nation of Israel. God didn't answer his plea to take his life, and we can imagine an awkward and persistent silence as Elijah grumbled his way through the wilderness. But here in the darkness of the cave, God spoke to him. *What are you doing here, Elijah?*

In response, Elijah complained of his thwarted efforts, and God called him out of hiding. But before he could even respond, the mountain erupted into an apocalyptic storm outside the cave, and Elijah wisely stayed put.

Henry comments further, "Those [signs] struck an awe upon him, awakened his attention, and inspired humility and reverence; but God chose to make known his mind to him in whispers soft, not in those dreadful sounds. When he perceived this, [Elijah] wrapped his face in his mantle, as one afraid to look upon the glory of God, and apprehensive that it would dazzle his eyes and overcome him. The angels cover their faces before God in token of reverence (Isaiah 6:2). Elijah hid his face in token of shame for having been such a coward as to flee from his duty when he had such a God of power to stand by him in it. The wind, and earthquake, and fire, did not make him cover his face, but the still voice did. Gracious souls are more affected by the tender mercies of the Lord than by his terrors."[3]

So it was that I was called out of my own hiding, not so much by the threefold terrors as by the gentle whisper of the Spirit.

I was hiding because I did not believe myself to be

worthy of love. In the stillness of that place, Jesus inquired, "Why are you hiding from me?"

"Have you not seen what I have done? I've hurt so many people. Even my best attempts to serve you well, I've failed you over, and over, and over again."

"Who told you that you have failed me?"

"As if anyone needed to tell me. Is it not obvious?"

"Come out from your hiding place and stand before me. Let me tell you what I see."

In the darkness of my cave, my eyes were unaccustomed to the Light, and my ears could only hear the echoes of my own thoughts. My performance-based view of acceptance caused my mind to race with doubts of inadequacy and failure, of shame and cowardice. But none of that was from God; that was all just a man in his prison cell. The world has a standard that we must live up to in order to be found worthy of love. But Grace tells a different story.

Matthew Henry continues:

"It is God's work to preserve that remnant, and distinguish them from the rest, for without his grace they could not have distinguished themselves: I have left me; it is therefore said to be a remnant according to the election of grace. . . . God's faithful ones are often his hidden ones (Psalms 83:3), and the visible church is scarcely visible, the wheat lost in the chaff and the gold in the dross, till the sifting, refining, separating day comes. The Lord knows those that are his, though we do not; he sees in secret. There are more good people in the world than some wise and holy men think there are. Their jealousy of themselves, and for God, makes them think the corruption is universal; but God sees not as they do. When we come to heaven, as we shall miss a great many whom we thought to meet there, so we shall meet a great many whom we little thought to find there.

God's love often proves larger than man's charity and more extensive."[4]

Because I was only able to perceive the external circumstances with my mind and had little or no awareness of the condition of my heart, I believed my tiny religion had rejected me. I was holding myself to its standards and found myself lacking, resolving that I must be unlovable. I was hiding out of discouragement, out of a deep knowledge that I was purposed for more, yet try as I might, I could not attain it. Just as Elijah was discouraged that God's people still did not turn back to Him, I tried time and again to muster up my own faith, to force my eyes to see God move. Not surprisingly, God revealed that's simply not how He works.

God moves in secret. His mission is to convince us of His unconditional love that continuously flows out of the fullness of His being. Religion tells us that if we muster up enough faith, we'll be able to hear His voice and see His hand moving. But the Spirit insists that we must first believe in order to see. In truth, the beginning of faith is the beginning of sight. Faith isn't built; it grows. It must be nurtured, and it cannot grow without the right conditions of the heart.

Like any good gardener, God goes to work breaking up the hardened soil of our hearts. This, of course, is not a quick and painless process, and it's only hindered by our reluctance to be tilled. Without the tilling, the soil cannot receive the seed. But if we accept His vision for our lives, if we succumb to the natural order set in motion at the beginning of time, we'll soon find our tender seedlings emerge back into the daylight, hungry for the light that will make us grow tall and strong. It's then that we'll scarcely remember the pain we felt when He sowed the seeds of faith into our hearts.

Faith, by definition, is letting go of our need to control things because we know that we are cared for. We know the

Spirit is at war with the flesh, and our illusion of control is very much enslaved within the flesh. As such, faith is not a natural disposition, it's a supernatural deposit.

Without it, we see what we see and we hear what we hear, regardless of the reality that what is said is said. Still, He speaks His love over us whether we receive it or not. And our good Master loves us too much to allow us to go our own way by the artificial light that the world conjures up. He does so because He is able to see from an infinitely higher perspective that our days will eventually become so dark that the only light we see is the true Light. It is undeniable.

IN MY OWN LIFE, GOD allowed me to retreat within myself to a place where I might be met and known by Him. Lying in the grave I'd dug for myself, there were no more distractions or fleeting illusions of progress and failure. I saw a pierced hand reach into my darkness and bring my heart back from the land of the dead. He brought me into His home and gave me food, water, clean clothes, and offered me rest.

My friends, this miracle does not just happen once and then we go on living in eternal bliss. This story happens multiple times every day as God rescues each and every broken place in our heart. And when His light falls on the various illusions that have taken our identities captive, their true nature is revealed, and we are happy to let them fall to the ground and shatter beneath us. Instead of some false life we can hold in our hands, our eyes are adjusted to see that true life cannot be contained or possessed. It simply is, and just as He invited Elijah to participate in His plan to rescue God's people, we, too, are invited to participate with God for the life of the world.

He sent Elijah back to where he had been running from with clear directions as to how he would participate in the glorification of God's name. So it is when God sends us back to the life we've been running from, it's by His love that we're now free and able to love other people well. We can tell the stories of how God's reckless love liberated us from captivity. The forgiveness and grace He showed us can now be extended to those around us. He knew us when we were still far off, and it's by His understanding that we can seek to understand the struggles of those around us. Understanding enables empathy. Empathy inspires compassion. Compassion, the compassion of Jesus, has the power to change the world.

Are you able to let go of the illusions of yourself that your mind constructs? Do you believe God is who He says He is? If so, do you believe what He says about you? I know how difficult and uncomfortable it is to be in that process, but would you believe Him if he told you that the very things you struggle against the most are the very things He wants to reshape for His glory? How, then, would you view your struggles, and how would you gauge that discomfort?

We all want to be free. We all desire to be seen and known by God, to be called His precious sons and daughters. God delights in giving us that desire, just as He delights in fulfilling it. We need new eyes.

SOMETIMES I'M OVERWHELMED AT the reality that I get to be Yonah's master. He's such an amazing dog and is, without a doubt in my mind, a precious and precise gift from the Lord. I love watching how he plays and interacts with the world, and he inspires me to do the same. He takes on my personality as we spend more and more time together. It reminds me of how we're all made in the image of our Father and continue to reflect Him more and more as we bask in His presence.

On our walks in the countryside, Yonah might disappear for fifteen to twenty minutes at a time, but he always checks back in. Even a year ago, he would be gone for a much longer period to the point of making me anxious about his well-being. I didn't knowingly train him to come back, it just developed out of our bond. To me, this means whatever curiosities are out there to be explored are ultimately not as important to him as keeping tabs on where I am.

It's really special to me, especially when juxtaposed with my relationship with Jesus. I don't have the whole omnipresent thing going for me like the Spirit, but I could imagine it being as if Yonah could, at any moment, turn around and see me smiling and joyfully sharing in his adventures. No matter where he could run, I'd always be just a few steps behind.

As my eyes are adjusting to the Light of an ever-present, death-defying Jesus, I'm learning He delights to be found in the seeking; there is nowhere He cannot be found. As long as our eyes desire to rest on Him, they will be satisfied.

This goes against everything I had previously believed about needing to clean up my act in order to walk with Jesus. I thought that I was supposed to be rid of sin so that I could go out and save the world, but I was wrong on both accounts. As I walk with Him in the present and openly discuss my past wounds, He reveals where He was in the midst of all those failures. Even though I couldn't see Him, He was there, and that knowledge is increasing my confidence and ability to trust He'll be every bit as present in my future.

I'm also learning that life is not about how much we can do for God, but about how much God has done in us. This transformation can only happen when Jesus trains our eyes to recognize what He has done and what He's doing in every moment. This transformation is profound, yet also elemental. All of creation glistens in the Light of the Creator, and eyes accustomed to this sight will recognize it as a continuous stream of life and eternally present wealth.

"Lord, make me an instrument of Thy peace;
Where there is hatred, let me sow love;
Where there is injury, pardon;
Where there is doubt, faith;
Where there is despair, hope;
Where there is darkness, Light;
Where there is sadness, joy.
Divine Master, grant that I may not so much seek to be
consoled, as to console;
To be understood, as to understand;
To be loved, as to love.
For it's in giving that we receive;
It's in pardoning that we are pardoned;
It's in dying to the self that we're born into eternal life
in Christ Jesus, our Lord.
Amen"[5]
— Saint Francis of Assisi,
thirteenth-century Catholic friar

When we're brought out of hiding, our fears of inadequacy are replaced with a renewed sense of purpose. As we receive strength for the task before us, the burden of shame is transformed into an eagerness to celebrate. We become acutely aware that our lives are no longer defined by our performance. We are surprised to find life is not about doing; it's about being, and being filled with the Spirit enables us to simply rest in His presence. That presence enables us to give as we have been given to, understand as we have been understood, love as we have been loved.

As Saint Francis points out, we are instruments of His divine peace, an extension of Himself through which He pours out His love unto His beloved. We recall all the Father has done and is still doing for us, how He meets us in our weakest moments when we prefer the loneliness of the wilderness. His gentle whisper penetrates the darkness of the cave and rouses our fearful, shame-filled hearts. We are called out to stand before Him, not that He may punish us, but that we may be seen and known by Him. He invites us deeper into the mystery of being made in His image. If we bear His resemblance, then, surely, we share in the desires of His heart. That heart cannot bear to see His children forget their true nature and become lost to themselves.

He longs to give life to a dead world, to see His children return from their perilous journey. He desires it so much that He waits for us with an eye to the horizon. When He sees us still far off in the distance, He runs to us with open arms. As our wearied bodies collapse into His strong embrace, His tears of joy mix with our tears of shame and he wipes them away with an adoring kiss and a cloak of honor.

I don't expect to ever understand how He loves us so, but my days of trying to figure that out are over. I'm learning to walk in stride with Jesus, and my heart is becoming attuned to the promptings of the Spirit. My old tendency to hide in shame is being replaced with a compulsion to celebrate out of gratitude. I often still wander off from the safety of His presence, but my eyes are quick to recognize the emptiness therein. By grace, I remember that bitter taste and come away to something sweet and refreshing.

Following Jesus looks wildly different from how I'd always pictured it. Admittedly, from the outside it looked boring and dull, but this could not be further from the truth. Following Jesus is a risky and daring adventure. It's mysterious, yet strangely familiar. It takes courage, resilience, firmness, and flexibility. It requires practice and discipline. We venture to far-off lands, and yet remain at home. Because

Jesus has established His Kingdom in our hearts, we carry our home along with us wherever we go.

As God brings people into our lives, they catch a glimpse of the Kingdom, and we're able to extend to them the same loving welcome that was shown to us. It's both liberating and empowering to know that each and every person we meet is longing to see their home. They are longing for the same acceptance we once sought after, and we know all too well the frustration, exhaustion, and confusion of not being able to understand why the world won't give it to them. They might not know they are looking for Jesus, but if they're looking for acceptance and we agree that can only be found in and through Jesus, they are, in truth, looking for Jesus. Perhaps they've even heard of Jesus and believe, as I once did, that they need to be better before they are worthy of His love. Jesus never insists that we be better; He only seeks to reveal that we are already immensely more precious than we could ever imagine. It brings me indescribable joy to look someone in the eye and tell them that I, too, went to great lengths to try to earn that acceptance, only to find I had always been accepted. Even when we are a long way off, our Father recognizes His children and runs to welcome us home.

Knowing that's what Jesus did for us and accepted us despite all the life we've squandered, we're free to reciprocate that gesture and accept someone no matter where they are in their journey. When we come to accept the people in our lives as they are, as Jesus does, there's a chance they might catch a glimpse of home in our eye. They may not yet have eyes to see it, but their hearts recognize something familiar. When they hear of our perilous journey and of the great Love that sought us out and rescued us from the wilderness, I assure you that story will go with them on their way. That's all that is required of us. We simply introduce them to the Jesus we're falling in love with, and Jesus will take it from there.

I feared this introduction for the longest time, mainly because I was focused on myself and on my own shortcomings. I was always hesitant to share my story because I know how littered it is with sin and regret. I was afraid how people might respond if they found out I was, and still am, full of flaws; I felt like a hypocrite attempting to help someone else when I couldn't even help myself. I concealed my wounds because I was afraid that the darkness I knew that was inside me would be let out and everyone would come to know me as the fake I was.

After I encountered Jesus—not the removed, storybook Jesus of my childhood but the real-life, ever-present Jesus who exists beyond my understanding—He revealed that my individual wounds were actually the fabric of my story. They were the place where the Light could enter into the darkness and expose their true nature as the harsh reality of fallen man.

What is this shame that we've come to associate with our wounds, and why do we go to such lengths to conceal their existence? When we first learned of our humanity as children, whenever we fell and skinned our knee, we might have cried at first, but that was out of a fear that something much worse had happened. After we realized it was just a boo-boo and a grownup kissed it to make it all better, we didn't hide the wound. In fact, we did just the opposite, often peeling off the bandage to flaunt our new prized possession!

"Look what happened! I got a boo-boo!" we'd say.

"Wow, you must be really tough, huh?" a grownup might kindly respond.

"Yeah, it didn't hurt that bad," completely forgetting the horror and pain we experienced in the moment of wounding.

The Thrill of the Hunt

Are we so different now? Have our basic human needs changed to where we no longer need another human being to acknowledge that we've been hurt? Are we, perhaps, now so scared of what that pain represents, that we're weak, unable to control the events of our lives and protect ourselves from the very thing that makes us human?

Or maybe we conceal and ignore our flaws because, deep within us, we know we were not made to experience them. We are somehow aware that we left our eternal home, where there no tears or pain, and we traveled to a far-off land riddled with both. We're tired of being gone, and we just want to go home. But we don't know the way. We need someone to walk with us and take us there. Who is equipped for such a task?

THE LATE IRISH WRITER AND poet, John O'Donohue, devoted the latter part of his life to the exploration and pursuit of beauty. His book *Beauty—The Invisible Embrace* opens our eyes and hearts to the infinite mystery we encounter every time we are in the presence of beauty. But his explanation of beauty is hardly limited to that which we'd find in a landscape, though his account of the Irish shoreline is more than enough reason to read the book. O'Donohue encourages his readers to engage in an intimate relationship with the many forms of beauty and suggests human suffering and woundedness are among those that might make the most profound imprint.

> "The beauty that emerges from woundedness is a beauty infused with feeling; a beauty different from the beauty of landscape and the cold beauty of perfect form. This is a beauty that has suffered its way through the ache of desolation until the words or music emerged to equal hunger and desperation at its heart. It must also be said that not

all woundedness succeeds in finding its way through to beauty of form. Most woundedness remains hidden, lost inside forgotten silence. Indeed, in every life there is some wound that continues to weep secretly, even after years of attempted healing. Where woundedness can be refined into beauty a wonderful transfiguration takes place. For instance, compassion is one of the most beautiful presences a person can bring to the world, and compassion is born from one's own woundedness. When you have felt deep emotional pain and hurt, you are able to imagine what the pain of the other is like; their suffering touches you. *This is the most decisive and vital threshold of the human experience and behavior.* The greatest evil and destruction arises when people are unable to feel compassion. The beauty of compassion continues to shelter and save our world. If that beauty were quenched, there would be nothing between us and the end-darkness which would pour in torrents over us."[6]

By O'Donohue's explanation, our woundedness does not have to be as oppressive as we so often make it out to be. How quick we are to hold ourselves hostage by our own victimization! On the contrary, if we loosen our grip, forgo the illusion of control, and seek the hidden beauty at the source of our pain, woundedness can be profoundly liberating. But herein lies the problem. We have to willingly let go. Our desires cannot be ripped away from us; they must be surrendered as an act of faith, trusting in things unseen rather than those dim objects to which our eyes have grown accustomed.

There it is again—a subtle shift in perspective that has the power to alter the imbalance of our lives. We come away from what we know for the hope of what we don't. Paradoxically, we trade in our faulty shells for the promise of further pain, only to find ourselves freed from the oppression of both. By entering into this mystery, our perspective of the flaws within and around us slowly dissolves into the natural rhythm of all things. O'Donohue suggests, "Once we recognize how control and self-protection rob life of all vitality and rhythm, we will find ourselves slowly advancing towards the threshold of risk and trust once more."[7]

Isn't it strange that when we insist that life go a certain way, we sabotage our own happiness and retreat within ourselves? Yet when we surrender our incessant need for understanding and control, our lives evaporate into an infinite sea of possibility, often carrying us to pleasures far beyond anything we could have conjured up on our own. From this perspective, the presence of a flaw becomes the very point where the frailty of creation intersects with the perfection of the Divine. This phenomenon elevates humanity out of its stagnant existence and reiterates the universal truth that life is defined by change. "If that beauty were quenched, there would be nothing between us and the end-darkness which would pour in torrents over us."

As our minds are rehabilitated from this flawed perspective, we embark upon the return journey home. Our lives still echo the same suffering of our past and present circumstances, yet they are illuminated by a different glow. Here, we can actually slow down and approach our surroundings with a renewed vitality. Here we can take refuge from the ever-looming illusion of progress. Here, we find that colors have a new vibrancy, and the light interacts with the shadows ever so slightly as to pique our interest in the most peculiar ways.

From this vantage point, our tired eyes are entertained by

observing the eternal as it entices the temporary. "We find that we are being gently rescued from the illusion of progress, and the fragile dimensions of the exiled soul begin to return." [8]

IN TRUTH, THE JOURNEY HOME began when we entered into this fallen world. Death was never intended to be a part of the human experience; now, this present reality cannot be explained apart from the existence of birth and death. Even still, we deceive ourselves when we believe these to be the isolated events that mark the beginning and end of our great adventure. Just as our days are measured by the rising and the setting sun, life invites us deeper into the constant flux of the eternal present moment.

As this moment ebbs and flows through the circumstances of our lives, our wholeness hangs in a balance of our own choosing. Will we insist that our own strength and understanding are sufficient to order the events of our lives in our favor, or would we cast off this burdensome illusion of control, knowing we have a Father in heaven that is exceedingly good and loves to provide for the needs of His children?

It's because of this great love that we are given the choice. The rest of creation doesn't have this choice; other living things of the earth *must* rely on their Creator to provide for them. But we choose moment by moment where we will look for our fulfillment. As much as we might think we grow out of childhood, we are and always will be helpless children. If we would only give up the illusion of progress, donning layer after layer of hardened shell to cover our nakedness, we might find that we're really just kids at heart playing dress-up for the world around us. When our needs are truly met by the fullness of Jesus's love and acceptance, we're free to enjoy everything else in gratitude.

The Thrill of the Hunt

I DON'T THINK IT'S COINCIDENTAL that God brought Yonah into my life when I was undergoing a rather dramatic shift in perspective. At a time when I was learning what it means to be a good master, to provide, to discipline, and to care for the needs of a helpless puppy, I also needed to learn what it means to have a good Master.

In all of my daily adventures with Yonah, I see a reflection of myself and the Father. Yonah knows the sound of my voice; his ears have been tuned to the shrill of my whistle. Upon hearing it, he comes bounding across the field with ears flopping in the wind and a big wet tongue slapping his cheek. Whenever this happens, I find myself beaming with pride and joy, knowing my Master is just over my shoulder smiling at the same thing.

It was, of course, not always this way. There was a time when I'd have to chase him down with my ears flopping in the wind and my tongue hanging out of the side of my mouth, panting from exhaustion. That's when I'd pick him up and stomp back to the house cursing at him, all the while Jesus was right there with us just laughing at the irony of the situation. But after the repetition of practice, we developed a bond secured by mutual trust, and I now rarely use either the leash or the e-collar that helped us get to this point.

This is all possible now because of a single rule I've put in place for Yonah's protection and for our well-being. The rule is simply this: listen to me. If Yonah obeys, he can go with me everywhere I go. If he doesn't, he's going to be spending a larger portion of his time in the kennel. This is not punishment, my friends. This is the reality of the situation. If he won't listen to me, then I can't trust him to be with me. I could, of course, put him on the leash, just as I'd be kept out of trouble if Jesus had me on a leash. But neither of us want that, and we'd much prefer to trust one another.

Jesus gave us a similar rule, though, a commandment put in place for our well-being.

"'*Love the Lord your God with all your heart and with all your soul and with all your mind.' This is the first and greatest commandment. And the second is like it: 'Love your neighbor as yourself.'*" (Matthew 22:37-39)

In short, He says, "*Follow me. Do as I do.*"

Jesus was and is Man fully alive, and He'll forever be unto the glory of the Living God. He is the Head, and those that follow Him are the members of His body, extending life unto the barren earth. As we surrender to this reality and respond to His invitation, God is glorified by His body and delights in raising us to life.

Just as I am training Yonah to be a more suitable companion for the life I live, so, too, does Jesus invite us into the fullness of His mysteriously human and Divine experience. He came to give us the abundance of the Life that was given to Him, and though He is now seated at the right hand of God the Father Almighty, His Spirit is forever moving us toward the destiny for which we were designed.

When I observe Yonah's extravagant adventures through the seemingly mundane world around him, I imagine all of creation coming alive to appease his curiosity. In the same way, Jesus is giving us new eyes to perceive all He designed for our enjoyment. His creation glistens with the newness of every moment in ways that our once-deadened hearts could not contain the abundance of the life we're all invited to experience.

At the conclusion of every adventure, our hearts are contented to lie at the feet of our Good Master. He has cared for us well, and we can now rest in the confidence of tomorrow's promise to bring a whole new world just waiting to be explored.

My writing partner.

Afterword

"I have done wrong. I've done wrong. I've done wrong, and that weight will follow me. But that weight is the world's. The world is not mine; it's the place where I am. And I have lost. I have lost. I have lost, and that won't let go of me. But that story's not me. It's who I can't change, and not who I can. No, that story's not me. It's who I can't change, and not who I am." [1]

— Aaron Nebeker of the band Blind Pilot

"[Jesus] called a little child to him, and placed the child among them. And he said: 'Truly I tell you, unless you change and become like little children, you will never enter the kingdom of heaven. Therefore, whoever takes the lowly position of this child is the greatest in the kingdom of heaven. And whoever welcomes one such child in my name welcomes me.'"

— Matthew 18:2-5

I OFTEN FIND MYSELF THINKING (and I'm sure you've heard someone say) that it must be nice to be a dog—playing and napping throughout the day, all the while their every need is met by its loving master. I wonder if we humans are not so different. Are we unable or unwilling to playfully enjoy our lives throughout every day and take rest in the knowledge that we are fully cared for by an all-powerful, all-knowing, all-loving Creator? Living life in this way would require a substantial amount of faith, and it's in the flux of

209

faith and doubt that our lives grow and are strengthened by the goodness and the faithfulness of God.

The whole time I've been writing this book, Yonah has been sitting in the chair next to me or at my feet, probably wondering what the hell I'm doing and why we're not outside playing. He has no idea I'm writing a book about him, about our time together and all the joy he brings into my life. I wonder if we ever do that with our Master, questioning where He is in the midst of our journey, unaware that He's right there with us, writing us into the pages of His story.

My FRIENDS, MY LIFE IS still a mess. I'm still utterly human. I still find myself frustrated, thinking I should be past a certain test of faith. But I'm reminded that I only see in part, and if I'm still experiencing a tension, then I'm still desperately in need of developing trust.

As our bond deepens, He's opened my eyes to the futility of living from a moral-centered perspective. That sort of relationship is restricted to the past tense with God, as if He said long ago, "*Do this; don't do that; follow all the rules and I'll reward you when you die.*" But what sort of life would that be? That's about like Yonah obeying the first rule I gave him when he came to my home at twelve weeks old and now I expect him to be an enjoyable companion to share my home with. That would be absurd, right? He's going to be miserable and he'd make me miserable, too.

But God loves us too much for that, and essentially says, "*Come, follow me, and I will teach you to hear and see me in all things. This way, you will know I am always by your side, and you may begin to truly see how much I love you.*" Learning to live with this constant grace, that's all present tense. We develop a bond and learn to trust in His goodness and listen to the sound of His Spirit whispering His love into our hearts.

Oh, how wonderful it is to be a child of God, so in need of grace every moment! How big a relief it is to know that grace is infinitely offered, readily available if I accept the fact that I'm hopeless without it. I still try on a daily basis to compensate for my insecurities and fears. I still seek life from lifeless things. But the gentle reminders of Jesus's love woven throughout the most minute of moments are more than enough to quickly remind me how small my problems are and how magnificent our Jesus is.

But no matter how messy my life is, I can always find more reasons for which to be thankful and praise our Master that there are things about which to complain. If we go through our lives insisting on perfection and maximum comfort, we're ironically going to be fixated on all the problems, pain, and discomfort. Think about it next time you're around someone who is constantly complaining. What are they complaining about—that life is not perfect and their expectations that it should be are being thwarted? All they can think about is their failed expectations, and they don't mind letting you know because they somehow believe it will alleviate their discomfort. But if we let go of that notion and truly accept the reality of our broken humanity and the promise of the Father, perhaps those pains and discomforts aren't quite as domineering.

If you want to be set free, you have to come into union with the One who never dies. You don't have to do anything but open your hands. Release your grip. Heaven came down to earth so you don't have to keep trying to get to heaven. Believe it. Receive it. Live from that place, and you just might find you have more than you could ever imagine. If our hands are full, we can't receive anything else. But if our hands are open, there's no limit to the gifts of grace, waiting just beyond our perception, that God longs to shower over us.

The Thrill of the Hunt

Understandably, my accident left me with more than a slight limp and a gnarly scar that runs more than half the length of my spine. The immense gift I was given as a catalyst for the healing in my heart has produced a deeper level of humility, which has in turn, resulted in gratitude. I'm becoming a child.

Believe it or not, my back is actually the part of my body that hurts least from the accident. After all, I have eight rods fused into my spine, and it's probably never been stronger. The immense blow from the five-story fall rippled throughout my body.

The padding in my feet blew out and I can no longer walk barefoot, which might sound petty, but it was a pleasure I'd grown quite fond of. My feet are now slightly deformed due to nerve damage, and doctors fear I'm well on my way to a severe case of claw feet, where my toes will eventually curl beneath me. My ankles, knees, and hips usually begin to ache on any given afternoon, and I'm eager to sit down except for the fact that sitting is by far the least comfortable position for my back. I can no longer stand for more than an hour or two at a time, and my sense of balance is laughable still. (I even have to lean against the wall to put on and take off my pants.)

Because of where the laceration occurred in my spinal cord injury, I also lost control of my bowel and bladder. I used catheters for the first year of my recovery and have since resorted to wearing diapers and excusing myself to the bathroom every hour or so. Even still, I have accidents often, which stopped being embarrassing after about the fifth accident. The frequency of my accidents has led me to wear black jeans on most occasions, as pissing your pants in black pants, as opposed to, say, khakis, could grant you at least a minute or more to calmly excuse yourself to the nearest set of dry pants.

I hope you'll join me in making light of the situation, and I beg you not to hear this as a list of complaints or a plea for sympathy. I only share them with you to illustrate the number of times throughout the day that I remember the healing that has taken place, not only in my physical body, but more importantly, in my heart.

Every painful step, I remember that I can walk. Every time I have a bowel or bladder accident, I'm grateful that I don't have to walk around with a bag full of either strapped to each leg. Every time I lie down, I'm grateful for the rest. No, all these serve as constant reminders that my heart still beats with the gift of life, and as often as the thought enters my mind, I'm eager to receive it, regardless of what it may or may not look like in a given moment. If that isn't grace, my friends, I simply don't know what is.

I'll tell you what else—my pain tolerance has certainly elevated itself. I often wonder if that's another gift of God allowing the pain and humiliation to do its work on my flesh, my ego, so that I might lower my guard and actually allow Him to speak His love into my heart.

This thought, along with the fact that I cannot control basic bodily functions, often makes me smile. It reminds me that life is a gift that should never be taken for granted. Furthermore, it reminds me of the immensity of God's love and how far He is willing to go to pursue His children and free them from the great illusion. It's true, I've not done this body of mine any favors with many of my reckless tendencies. But you can bet your bottom dollar on the day I turn this old life suit in for a brand new heavenly body, I'll be hollering up all sorts of hallelujahs.

I also now have a fascinating medical condition known as Cauda Equina Syndrome (CES). Many of my symptoms are understandably due to nerve damage in the bundle of nerves at the end of the spinal cord called the *cauda equina*. *Cauda* means *tail*, and *equina* means *horse*. Our nervous system descends from the brain through our spinal cord, but when it reaches the area above the tailbone, it spreads out through our pelvis, resembling a horse tail, which is obviously where the name comes from.

Nerves are very complex and no one can say for sure whether I'll recover from any of this damage. I find this uncertainty especially fascinating. The way the nerves travel in a singular cord and then sort of fray out into the oblivion of our bodies is beautifully symbolic of our own awakening. Our minds proceed in a singular focus under the illusion of control until they have an encounter with the Eternal. After that encounter dissolves any notion of control, we come to the end of ourselves and are immersed into the mystery of life's grandeur and the boundlessness of life's possibilities.

I know that can be a terrifying thought, the process of surrendering our control, but maybe it helps to remember that we never had it in the first place. Realizing that we no longer need anything from the world, we can give up our vain attempts to manipulate it. The world has nothing to offer us that our Father has not already provided, and yet, we now have everything to offer it. That, my friends, is the sort of beautiful mystery I was seeking my whole life and one that I will gladly rest in for the rest of my days. I pray you'll find a way to do the same.

As you press into your own mystery before you, I encourage you to share the journey with the people around you. It's a wonderful way to seek healing, acceptance, and the miracle of grace with the people God brings into our lives. To echo O'Donohue, "This is the most decisive and vital threshold of the human experience and behavior."[2] The more we share, we'll quickly find how similar our struggles are.

They might manifest themselves in different ways, but they are truly all the same at their core. The remedy for this pain is not in the subsiding of the symptoms; it's in the confidence that, despite the pain, we can hold to the promise that Jesus has overcome the world and has established His kingdom within our hearts. There is nowhere else to go.

For the longest time, I wanted Jesus to wipe away my past, but doing so would also wipe away what Jesus had done in it and how He gracefully led me to discover my moment-by-moment need for Him. I now carry my mat with pride and tell the story of His Love as often as possible. I tell of all the times I felt lost and alone, of my deepest fear of life vanishing into the fray of meaninglessness. I tell of how Jesus met me there and told me that I was never alone, nor could I ever be alone. Nothing could separate me from His great love. I'm still very much in the fray of the unknown, but I'm no longer afraid.

Thankfully, God gives us spiritual gifts to help us navigate the mystery. He delights in giving good gifts to His children, and it's a way God allows Himself to be found in the seeking. Like the time in Hawaii when I first knowingly encountered the Spirit, I engaged Him through the gift of tongues. I don't know what I was saying, and in truth, it doesn't really matter. It came at a time when I deeply needed to feel God's embrace. It's similar to the way Elijah prayed for the Spirit of God to show up in a very visible and apparent way. God doesn't always need to send a fireball from heaven to prove His powerful existence, just like I don't need to chant in tongues and be drenched in sweat for me to feel the embrace of the Spirit. That was a gift that I needed in a moment of longing, but the true gift came from the awareness that the Spirit can be engaged in the slightest of moments. It's the simple shift in perspective that the Spirit of Jesus is here and now, not when and then, as our minds so often lead us to believe. He is very much here and is more than enough to provide our hearts the acceptance and fullness that we so long for if we're willing to turn our attention to Him.

(Oh, and by the way, God never answered Elijah's prayer to end his life. He was actually swept up by a fiery chariot and taken to heaven in a whirlwind. How's that for disappearing into the fray!)

I still have plenty of places in my heart that I don't trust God to be enough for me. The journey of discovering our true identity is certainly not without its perils, but we can take hope in the process, knowing it's the only true passage to the destination for the longing in our hearts. We have another saying at our church that we'd all do well to remember often, acknowledging that faith is not a natural disposition, it's a supernatural deposit. Faith, like all spiritual gifts, is not something we can muster up; it first and foremost must be received from our loving Father. Then, through the process of trial and the repetition of our doubts being met by God's faithfulness, our faith is developed. We begin to notice many of the other gifts we've been equipped with for the journey ahead. These gifts reflect the various faces of the Father's Divine nature, and He takes great pleasure in both revealing them to us as well as nurturing them inside of us.

There's something in our fallen nature that seems to undermine the very things we want most in life—freedom, acceptance, love, and joy. Life is about honesty. It's about admitting that we are human, that we are not capable of providing for ourselves the things we want. And guess what? We don't have to because we have a Father in heaven, a Good Master, who deeply cares for us and about us and longs for us to participate in the life and the love that He has spoken over us from the beginning of time.

There's a language that's hardwired into who we are. There's a language of our soul that God is speaking to us, and the reason we might feel detached from it is not because He's not speaking, not because we're not worthy or because we haven't done enough. Perhaps we don't hear His voice because we're hiding from who we are at depths of our being. We are fearfully and wonderfully made and known by God, and in the Light of His Love, we don't have to suffer under the burden of humanity. Instead, we are invited to explore the beautiful intricacies of our humanity as children of God. We can only do that when we are willing to come away from whatever ideas we have about ourselves and who we're supposed to be. It's in this place that we are invited to simply come and rest at the feet of our Master.

Yonah pointing at sparrows downtown.

One too many dog beers.

Afterword

Yonah's first snow.

The Thrill of the Hunt

Where Yonah learned to swim.

Yonah chasing sandpipers at Fripp Island.

Notes

Chapter 1: Puppyhood

1. Kephart, Horace. *Our Southern Highlanders*. Knoxville, Tennessee: University of Tennessee Press. 1976, p. 80.

Chapter 2: Discipline as Love

1. Giacopelli, Pablo. *Holding On Loosely: Finding Life in the Beautiful Tension*. Traveler's Rest, South Carolina: True Potential, Inc. 2011, p. 23.

Chapter 3: Training

1. Giacopelli, Pablo. *The Modern Fig Leaf: Uncovering Your True Identity*. Shippensburg, Pennsylvania: Destiny Image Publishers, 2015, p. 52.

Chapter 4: Bird's Eye View

1. Merton, Thomas. *The Seven Storey Mountain*. New York: Harcourt Brace and Company, 1948, p. 186.

Chapter 5: The Perils of Adventure

1. Gibran, Kahlil. *The Collected Works*. New York: Everyman's Library, 2007, p. 127.
2. McConnell, Patricia B. Ph.D. *The Other End of the Leash*. New York: Ballantine Books, 2002, p. 162.

Chapter 6: The Freedom of Boundaries

1. Lewis, C. S. *The Problem of Pain*. New York: The Macmillan Company, 1946, p. 22.
2. Ibid., p. 23.

3. Ibid., p. 30.
4. Gibran, Kahlil. *The Collected Works*. New York: Everyman's Library, 2007, p. 131.
5. Ibid., p. 485.

Chapter 7: The Joy of the Master

1. Lewis, C. S. *The Problem of Pain*. New York: The Macmillan Company, 1946, p. 23.
2. Merton, Thomas. T*he Seven Storey Mountain*. New York: Harcourt Brace and Company, 1948, p. 123.

Chapter 8: Oh, How Far We've Come

1. Keller, Timothy. *The Meaning of Marriage*. New York: Penguin Books, 2011, p. 73.
2. Henry, Matthew. *Matthew Henry Commentary on the Whole Bible*. Peabody, Massachusetts: Hendrickson Publishers. 1996. Vol 2.
3. Ibid.
4. Ibid.
5. Easwaran, Eknath. *Love Never Faileth*. Tomales, California: Nilgiri Press, 1984, p. 20.
6. O'Donohue, John. *Beauty—The Invisible Embrace*. New York: HarperCollins Publishers, 2004, p. 180-181.
7. Ibid., p. 181.
8. Ibid., 184.

Afterword:

1. Blind Pilot. Lyrics to "Which Side I'm On." Blindpilot.com, 2016, http://www.blindpilot.com/atll-lyrics.
2. O'Donohue, John. *Beauty—The Invisible Embrace*. New York: HarperCollins Publishers, 2004, p. 181.

Author Bio

ROB CRAWFORD LIVES IN KNOXVILLE, Tennessee, with his dog, Yonah. Rob studied film & television at Savannah College of Art & Design. He now works as a senior copywriter for Tombras Advertising and as communications director for Maker City Church, both of which are based in Knoxville.